Ancient Israel

A Captivating Guide to the Ancient Israelites, Starting From their Entry into Canaan Until the Jewish Rebellions against the Romans

© **Copyright 2018**

All Rights Reserved. No part of this book may be reproduced in any form without permission in writing from the author. Reviewers may quote brief passages in reviews.

Disclaimer: No part of this publication may be reproduced or transmitted in any form or by any means, mechanical or electronic, including photocopying or recording, or by any information storage and retrieval system, or transmitted by email without permission in writing from the publisher.

While all attempts have been made to verify the information provided in this publication, neither the author nor the publisher assumes any responsibility for errors, omissions or contrary interpretations of the subject matter herein.

This book is for entertainment purposes only. The views expressed are those of the author alone and should not be taken as expert instruction or commands. The reader is responsible for his or her own actions.

Adherence to all applicable laws and regulations, including international, federal, state and local laws governing professional licensing, business practices, advertising and all other aspects of doing business in the US, Canada, UK, or any other jurisdiction is the sole responsibility of the purchaser or reader.

Neither the author nor the publisher assumes any responsibility or liability whatsoever on the behalf of the purchaser or reader of these materials. Any perceived slight of any individual or organization is purely unintentional.

Contents

INTRODUCTION 1
CHAPTER 1 – CULTURE AND SOCIETY THROUGH THE YEARS 4
    GOVERNMENT AND ADMINISTRATION 4
    BUILDING AND ARCHITECTURE 6
    FOOD 7
    GENDER ROLES 12
    CLOTHING 13
CHAPTER 2 – THE LATE BRONZE AGE AND EARLY IRON AGE (1600 BCE – 1000 BCE) 15
    WHERE WERE THE ISRAELITES? 16
CHAPTER 3 – THE LATE IRON AGE (1000 BCE – 587 BCE) 20
    ISRAEL 20
    JUDAH 23
CHAPTER 4 – THE ISRAELITES UNDER BABYLON 27
    BEFORE THE NEO-BABYLONIAN EMPIRE 27
    THE NEO-BABYLONIAN EMPIRE 29
    REBELLION AND THE CREATION OF YEHUD 32
CHAPTER 5 – THE CONTROL OF THE PERSIANS 34
    THE BATTLE OF OPIS 35

The Israelites and the Persians 36

Persian Influence on Language, Literature, and Religion 37

The Fall of the Achaemenid Empire in the Levant 39

The Israelites under Alexander the Great... 42

CHAPTER 6 – THE HELLENISTIC PERIOD AND JUDEA UNDER THE SELEUCIDS 43

Hellenization and Antiochus IV 45

Maccabean Revolt... 47

CHAPTER 7 – THE EARLY HASMONEAN DYNASTY 50

Alexander Balas... 52

Jonathan's Rule.. 53

The Leadership of Simon 58

CHAPTER 8 – THE HASMONEAN EXPANSION AND CIVIL WAR 60

John Hyrcanus 60

The Successors of John Hyrcanus.. 63

The Pharisees and Sadducees 65

Hasmonean Civil War 66

CHAPTER 9 – ROMAN RULE OF JUDEA.. 70

The Fall of the Hasmonean Dynasty... 70

Herod and Continued Roman Control 72

Control and the Jewish-Roman Wars.. 74

CHAPTER 10 – ANCIENT HEBREW RELIGION AND JUDAISM........... 76

Monotheism vs. Polytheism 77

Yahweh.. 77

Israelite Religion and the Assyrians 81

Practices 82

CONCLUSION 84

READ MORE CAPTIVATING HISTORY BOOKS ABOUT ANCIENT HISTORY 86

BIBLIOGRAPHY 91

Introduction

The Israelites were an intriguing people and not quite what many would expect. They created the foundation of contemporary Judaism but practiced a separate culture and beliefs heavily influenced by the environment in which they lived. After all, no ancient civilization developed in a vacuum and most borrowed ideas, practices, and even entire languages from one another. It's therefore important to recognize the Israelites not only as the forefathers of Judaism, but also as a distinct group with many differences.

The Israelites originated in and lived around a region known as the Levant, which covered the territory of the modern countries of Cyprus, Israel, Iraq, Jordan, Lebanon, Palestine, Syria, and Turkey. The Israelites built their home along the eastern shore of the Dead Sea, in the location of modern Israel. This is an arid area; climate greatly affected the food and animals possessed by the Israelites.

The Modern Middle East

Israelites primarily lived during years which will be labeled BCE, or Before Common Era. This term refers to years that occurred before the start of the contemporary Gregorian calendar. Different names are used to refer to the Israelite homeland, but all these designations pertain to the same group of people living in distinct kingdoms over the centuries. These kingdoms include Israel, Judah, and Judea. The people will also be referred to by different terms to correlate with changing naming conventions over the centuries, including the Israelites, Judans, Judeans, and Jews.

The Israelites were unable to cling to their own kingdoms for long. Instead, they continued to be dominated by far more powerful empires in all directions, including the Babylonians, Persians, and Greeks. The Israelites primarily concentrated on the western shore of the Mediterranean Sea, in the location of modern-day Israel. They possessed two kingdoms at their highest point in history–Israel and Judah–and the main city was Jerusalem. They also developed their own religion, which began as the polytheistic worship of the royal family's patron deity and would eventually become a monotheistic religion that praised a single supreme being. Israelite culture would evolve along these religious lines, to the point where the Israelites believed they were God's chosen people.

Unlike many other ancient peoples, the culture and beliefs of the Israelites exist in modern society. They managed to survive through wars, persecution, and numerous revisions and adaptations caused by new invaders or internal rebellions. Because of their significance in contemporary society, it's important to learn more about the Israelites in order to fully understand how they developed and managed to contribute so heavily to the current culture of the Western world.

Chapter 1 – Culture and Society through the Years

Israelite society developed over millennia but managed to maintain some consistencies through the years. For example, the Israelites were patriarchal and the majority of the population were farmers, shepherds, or general laborers. Kings, nobles, and other wealthy men controlled politics and the development of an administrative government, and the Israelites were frequently at war with their neighbors over territory and resources. The main way they distinguished themselves from other cultures in the Levant was through their religion, which involved the worship of a single god believed to protect the Israelites as a people. This practice mirrored others in the area as, by the Iron Age, most of the kingdoms in the Levant possessed a patron god in charge of protecting a chosen people–always the people who just so happened to inhabit the kingdom.

Government and Administration

After living as members of other societies for centuries, the Israelites eventually formed the kingdoms of Israel and Judah. Both featured a hereditary monarchy ruled by the sons of the previous generation. The people believed the royal families descended from holy lines chosen and blessed by the kingdom's god, which gave the monarch the divine right to rule. A class of warrior aristocrats supported the monarchy by supplying well-trained soldiers in exchange for swathes of land owned and controlled by the aristocrat's family.

Unlike a lot of monarchies of the period, that of the Israelites was religiously motivated to the extreme. The Israelites believed that the king ruled as the viceroy for Yahweh, their deity. He therefore needed to uphold religious law and behave in a strict manner. Since the religion was additionally based on Yahweh making covenants or contracts with the Israelites, the king was the person who enforced these covenants and made sure the kingdom upheld the laws of Yahweh.

Other significant positions in the royal court were those of the scribe and cupbearer. The scribe was a crucial administrative figure responsible for managing judicial and accounting affairs for the king. The cupbearer filled the monarch's wine glass and brought it to him, preventing poisonings and other potential tampering. Lesser figures served as other administrators or scribes lower in the hierarchy. Some positions like governors collected taxes and ensured laws were enforced outside of the kingdoms' capitals.

Other important figures at this time were the priests. Unlike other cultures, the Israelites possessed a hereditary priest class where only members of specific families could take on a religious role. The priests, prophets, and preachers all served to keep the sovereign government in check and frequently ensured the covenants were followed. Many denounced various Israelite kings over the centuries for sins like worshipping other gods, the worship of idols, or sacrificing at the wrong temples. Women could not be priests, nor could they be administrators or warriors. From the Israelites' humble origins until the age of Roman rule, only two women would ever rise to the role of ruling monarch of an Israelite kingdom.

As time went on, the king would frequently also be the High Priest, or the main religious official of the Israelite faith. Several hereditary dynasties would come and go, all centered on the idea of being

God's chosen rulers. These included the Davidic and Hasmonean Dynasties, both of which will be discussed later.

Building and Architecture

The earliest ancestors of the Israelites were either nomads or lived in simplistic dwellings made of clay bricks, wooden posts, and thatched ceilings. Nomadic peoples preferred tents crafted from leather or cloth. Since the Levant is a warm, arid region, most dwellings needed to protect inhabitants from the wind and sun rather than snow or rain, so buildings were often open and shady.

Not much is known about the architecture of the Israelites during the Bronze Age and early Iron Age because the Israelites were not yet a distinctive people. Instead, many belonged to nearby peoples, including the Hittites, Canaanites, and Hurrians. The architecture of these locations continued to be simplistic but stone became more common, especially for administrative buildings and palaces. Large, public buildings like temples received the most attention and typically featured carved reliefs, pillars, and murals of the various deities worshipped by the people.

The most well-preserved examples of Israelite architecture come from the late Iron Age. Professionals discovered entire cities at archaeological sites in ancient Israel and Judah, including Tell Beit Mirsim, Tell el-Nasbeh and Tell el-Farah. Some defining characteristics include stone walls around the entire perimeter of the town, clay or stone houses with multiple rooms and open windows, and large public buildings constructed using chiseled stone blocks. The standard residence featured walls built from rubble, covered in mud, and then painted with lime to create a clean finish. Most people continued to keep animals in their homes if they had them, but the sleeping area for humans became separate.

One building style which emerged during this period involved building two separate stone layers to form a wall and using more flexible wood in between to bolster the structure and prevent damage during natural disasters. Stone ceilings were not used as they were too heavy. Instead, the Israelites continued to use thrushes and reeds, though logs would be added for larger, more important buildings.

Stone carvings and reliefs continued to be popular in Israelite dwellings from the Bronze Age throughout the entire Iron Age. Reliefs depicted deities, notable figures, or scenes from common myths. They gradually shifted from being simplistic to more detailed as the Israelites switched from bronze to iron tools that were stronger and capable of doing more intricate work.

Food

The ancient Israelite diet mirrored that of other peoples living in the Levant.[1] The main staples were bread, wine, and olive oil, which would be the standard fare a person would eat for every meal. Depending on the season, the Israelites additionally had access to fruits and vegetables such as leeks, onions, garlic, muskmelon, grapes, figs, olives, dates, apricots, and black radishes. Dandelion greens were not cultivated but could be foraged during the proper season and helped supplement a carbohydrate-rich diet. All parts of the dandelion can be eaten, even when the yellow turns fluffy, making them a common source of nutrition during lean years.

---

[1] Nathan MacDonald, *What Did the Ancient Israelites Eat?: Diet in Biblical Times* (Grand Rapids: Wm. B. Eerdmans Publishing Co., 2008).

Delicious Dandelion Greens

Fruit played a more significant role in the Israelite diet than vegetables. The Israelites mainly ate figs, olives, and grapes, which all grew consistently. Figs were eaten as they matured, as were pomegranates, apricots, and dates. Grapes could be eaten, but tended to be used to make wine for drinking. Many ancient peoples transformed grapes to wine because it was safer to drink than regular water sources. The majority of manufactured wine was watered down, especially compared to modern variants. Grapes not eaten immediately or fermented could be dried to make storable raisins, or they could be crushed. The crushed grapes would be drained of water and slowly turned into something called grape syrup or honey, which was used to sweeten foods. Dates could also undergo this process to produce date honey, which served the same purpose.

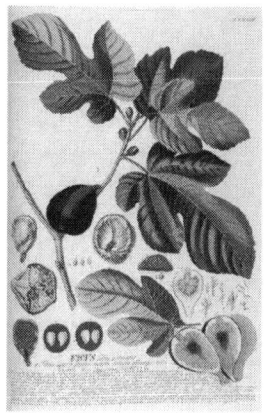

The Common Fig

Olives could be eaten fresh but were frequently pressed to form olive oil, which could be stored or eaten with bread. Olives formed an important part of life not associated with cooking and eating, including serving as a popular sacrificial offering, the making of ointments, and even lighting. The Israelites made huge strides in the development of olive oil. An archaeological site at Ekron, an ancient city, holds a several millennia-old olive production center which contains over 100 presses designed to make oil. In fact, the Israelites produced so much oil that they regularly traded it to nearby civilizations in the Levant, and even as far south as Egypt.

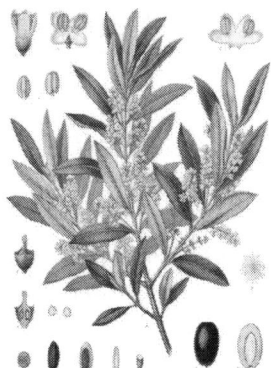

Olives

Vegetables were not held in esteem by the Israelites. It is difficult to find records or archaeological evidence demonstrating that they were being eaten because most vegetables were either boiled or eaten raw. Sometimes records indicate vegetables were a delicacy only the rich consumed since they required dedicated land to grow, but more often than not they were associated with poorer classes since they needed to be foraged. Most agricultural land was instead used to grow grains to make bread.

The Israelites grew two separate grains: barley and wheat.[2] While many people in the modern United States and Europe typically eat wheat bread, barley was the most important grain for ancient peoples and served as a major food. For the Israelites, barley was so important that an offering of fresh barley flour was, and continues to be, offered on the second day of Passover, and fields were measured by how much barley could be grown rather than wheat.

Barley

The making of bread was a time-consuming, backbreaking task performed by the women of a household. After the harvest of the grains, women would spend three hours every day grinding or milling enough grain to make enough loaves of bread to feed their families. Most grain was ground using a mortar and pestle or a grindstone, which involved crushing the grains between two rocks until it formed fine flour. Once the flour was prepared, women would mix in a starter. Women made the starter by saving a portion

---

[2] Ibid.

of the bread dough from the last day's batch and leaving it to sit out in the open. It would gather yeast from the air which helped the bread making process. This starter gave every loaf of bread a distinctive sourdough taste.

Before and during the early Iron Age, the Israelites baked bread with a jar oven or a pit oven. In the jar oven, fuel was heated inside and the dough cooked along the side of the jar, eventually forming bread. In a pit oven, a jar was lowered into the ground and fuel heated inside of it. The dough would go in the jar with the fuel and bake. Eventually, the Israelites started placing a platter on top of the jar and baking on that instead, which kept the ashes out of the bread.

Later, Persians introduced the tandoor, which cooked in a manner similar to the pit oven but without leaving ashes in the food. All of the bread produced using these methods was thin and malleable, and eaten by dipping it into sauces, gravy, or some form of liquid. The Romans introduced a more traditional oven which created thicker loaves. The Israelites seasoned the bread with fennel or cumin for flavor and would also dip it in olive and sesame oil. Sometimes honey was used to make the loaves sweeter, since plain barley loaves were notably bland.

Legumes were the final food group eaten by the Israelites and also one of the most significant. Archaeologists estimate that the Israelites ate legumes as 17% of their diet, and the food category was the main source of their protein. Some common legumes included lentils, field peas, bitter vetch, chickpeas, and broad or fava beans. Different legumes were consumed by the various social classes, with the poorest being forced to eat bitter vetch, which required being boiled multiple times to eliminate the acerbic taste. Other legumes like lentils could be ground or toasted into a dish similar to falafel. Lentils and beans frequently made their way into stews, where they would be roasted and seasoned with garlic, onions, and leeks.

Bitter Vetch

Gender Roles

Like many other ancient civilizations in the Levant, the Israelites possessed a deeply patriarchal society that separated roles for men and women. Property was typically owned by men and only men could become influential administrators and scribes. They could also enter into contracts with one another and many were expected to become soldiers or enter into military service. Most men learned trades at a young age from their father, which could range from being a farmer to an artisan to a blacksmith. Others became doctors, lawyers, judges, or influential religious figures like priests and scholars. Only wealthy men learned to read and write, since literacy would not be considered an important skill for the average farmer.

Women controlled the domestic sphere and possessed tremendous influence over household resources and finances. The majority of a grown woman's day was spent transforming raw materials like wool and grain into usable goods like textiles and flours for bread. This was backbreaking work, as noted earlier, and took many hours. Women additionally held responsibility for childcare, cooking, and cleaning. Some women became important medical professionals like midwives and herbalists, while others could become unofficial preachers since the Israelite religion banned female priests. Like young boys, young girls were taught by their mother from a young age and assisted in daily chores to become more skilled and prepared for their lives as eventual wives and parents. Upper-class women could enter into contracts and own property while also learning to read and write.

Clothing

Clothing played an important role in determining a person's social class; more specifically, people could tell how wealthy an individual was based on the type of clothes they wore. The majority of the population possessed simple wool clothes woven by the women of each household. The wool primarily came from sheep, and most families had at least one animal which would be shorn yearly to gather supplies for the family's clothes. Dyes were an expensive luxury, so the majority of clothing produced was the plain color of wool, usually a dirty brown or grey.

The wealthy could afford fabrics like linen, which traders imported from Egypt or gathered in prosperous Galilee. Aristocrats and rich administrators also had access to a variety of dyes. The most expensive was a specific purple color produced by manufacturing the murex snail, but cheaper violets were achieved by leeching the color from flowers like the hyacinth. Colors could even be derived from crushed insects, walnuts, and golden plants. White clothes were reserved for nobles who could afford to keep them clean by bleaching the garments in the sun and then scrubbing them down with a mix of vinegar, urine, and caustic soda. Expensive clothing frequently featured embroidery as well, especially when worn by the nobility.

Hyacinth Flowers

Almost all people wore a basic tunic, which was made by sewing two squares of fabric together and leaving holes for the head and arms. Cloaks or mantles were larger pieces of cloth that covered the tunic and added extra protection from the weather. Most featured pins or knots that held the mantle together at the shoulder, although the wealthy once again possessed fancier variations. Women tended to wear a veil which covered their hair and part of their face to preserve modesty. Israelites could identify prostitutes easily because these women went without veils. Men additionally covered their heads, usually with long rectangles of fabric held in place by wooden or cord circlets.

One unique characteristic of male clothing was the addition of tassels or a fringe on the corners of garments. These tassels supposedly reminded men to keep to their religious commandments and follow the laws of their god. Finally, all people except the very poor wore sandals of some kind. Almost all shoes were open-toed. The base could be made of wood or leather, and leather straps wrapped through and around the toes to keep the shoe on the foot. Archaeologists have found some closed-toe boots, but these seemed to be reserved for the wealthy.

Chapter 2 – The Late Bronze Age and Early Iron Age (1600 BCE – 1000 BCE)

Israelite society can be traced back to something known as the Bronze Age. This was a historical period characterized as a time when humans and civilizations made tools and weapons from bronze.[3] People additionally possessed some form of proto-writing, usually symbols with specific meanings, and had the beginnings of urban civilizations built around central cities.

The Israelites emerged during the Late Bronze Age, which lasted from roughly 1600 BCE to 1200 BCE and indicated a time when metalworking with bronze was more sophisticated, but on its way out. Indeed, the region from which the Israelites originate was one of the first areas around the world to learn metalworking with bronze, as seen on the map below. The Levant is one of the darker, copper-colored sections of the map on the right side of the Mediterranean. Unlike other cultures which needed to learn metalworking and writing for themselves, the Israelites borrowed heavily from the civilizations which came before or developed around them.

---

[3] Eric H. Cline, *1177 B.C.: The Year Civilization Collapsed* (New Jersey: Princeton University Press, 2014).

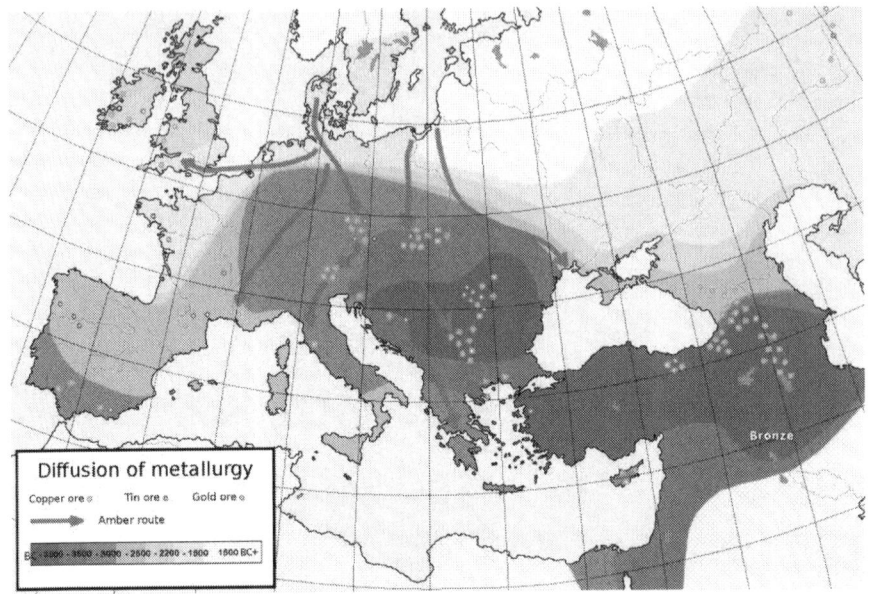

Metallurgical Diffusion during the Bronze Age

Where Were the Israelites?

Historians can trace the Israelites to a time so far back in history that they were not even known by the same name and weren't a separate ethnic group. Instead, they were members of a civilization known as Canaan, or the Canaanites. Canaan was a civilization that primarily existed during the Bronze Age before succumbing to the Bronze Age Collapse that destroyed many of the civilizations throughout the Levant. Originally tribes and groups of nomads, the Canaanites eventually formed a series of city-states located around modern Israel and Syria.

Some people might have heard of the Canaanites from the Old Testament, where they are listed as pagans, heathens, baby eaters, and overall unsavory characters. They did have separate gods from the Israelites, but many historians believe a good portion of their bad reputation comes from the fact that they continued to be a rival of the Israelites for food, territory, trade routes, and general survival in the Levant.

Archaeologists and historians possessed little evidence about the exact location and nature of Canaan until the late 20th century, when new dig sites revealed the civilization's clear boundaries. Like the Israelites, the Canaanites were a Semitic-language speaking group of people. They were polytheistic and shared many of their deities, linguistic patterns, diet, and other characteristics with their neighbors. Canaan even held its own against Egypt, which dominated Mesopotamia through its superior population and military technology.

However, the civilization could not last. The Bronze Age Collapse thoroughly devastated Canaan. This collapse occurred around 1200 BCE and could have happened for a variety of reasons. Historians speculate that the entire area crumbled due to invaders with better military equipment and strategies, devastating climate change that spawned earthquakes and poor crop harvests, the invasion of the Sea Peoples, and even general systems collapse.[4] Under the theory of general systems collapse, numerous factors made it more economically efficient for peasants to purchase weapons rather than expensive food, overthrowing the warrior aristocracy and spawning generations of raiders and bandits. The Sea Peoples were mysterious invaders who came from across the Mediterranean Sea and trounced the forces of existing states like Canaan.

The Sea Peoples

---

[4] Ibid.

Faced with so many problems, the Canaanite civilization slowly disintegrated into separate ethnic or cultural groups like the Phoenicians, Philistines, and Israelites. The Israelites existed for a period of time as wanderers or citizens of various settlements throughout the former territory of Canaan. The official term "Israel" doesn't appear in living record until the creation of the Merneptah Stele, which was inscribed by the servants of Pharaoh Merneptah of the 19th Egyptian Dynasty. Several important lines relate to the presence of the Israelites and the fate of the Canaanites:

"The princes are prostrate, saying, 'Peace!'

Not one is raising his head among the Nine Bows.

Now that Tehenu (Libya) has come to ruin,

Hatti is pacified;

The Canaan has been plundered into every sort of woe:

Ashkelon has been overcome;

Gezer has been captured;

Yano'am is made non-existent.

Israel is laid waste and his seed is not;

Hurru is become a widow because of Egypt."[5]

Since Israel was not a political state at this time, historians believe the reference is to the Israelites as a people, who formed a specific ethnic group based off of the Canaanites and other peoples in the Levant. There is little archaeological evidence to suggest a war or military conflict. Instead, it is likely that Egypt sought to suppress the Israelites as they did with the surrounding peoples and chose to list them among their conquered enemies since the Israelites possessed significant population numbers. It was around this time

---

[5] Kenton L. Sparks, *Ethnicity and Identity in Ancient Israel*, (Eisenbrauns: 1998).

that the Israelites joined the rest of the Levant in the transition to the Iron Age.

Chapter 3 – The Late Iron Age (1000 BCE – 587 BCE)

The Late Iron Age, also called Iron Age II, was a period of significant advancement from 1000 BCE to 587 BCE during which the kingdoms of Israel and Judah thrived. One of the key factors in this development was two centuries of unusually favorable climate conditions and changes which brought fruitful harvests, temperate weather, and spurred a massive population boom. New settlements popped up throughout the area and trade routes started to move exotic goods into both kingdoms.

Israel

In Israel, the city of Samaria emerged as a strong player in the Middle East. The city appeared to be so prosperous that it drew the attention of Egypt. An inscription created by Pharaoh Shoshenq I indicates that Egypt led several military campaigns against Samaria during the early centuries of Iron Age II. By the middle of the 9th century BCE, Israel appeared to be fighting against several of its neighbors for control of resource-rich regions, including the famous Jezreel Valley and Galilee. Their two main enemies for this territory were Damascus and Tyre, two major cities. All three players desired Jezreel Valley because it formed one of the easiest places for traders to travel across the Levant. It was thus the s of numerous battles, many of which Israel lost against its more powerful neighbors.

The Ruins of Samaria

Other military struggles came from the Assyrians of the Neo-Assyrian Empire and the kingdom of Moab, which was just across the Dead Sea from Israel. Israel was one of the eleven kingdoms that fought against the powerful Assyrian king Shalmaneser III in the Battle of Qarqar.[6] Fought in 853 BCE, the Battle of Qarqar possessed the greatest number of combatants seen in any military conflict in the region and was also the first instance where numerous peoples were recorded, including the Arabs. The leaders of the coalition of eleven kingdoms were King Hadadezer of Aram Damascus (a kingdom located around the city of Damascus) and King Ahab of Israel, demonstrating how important the kingdom was becoming in the area.

---

[6] Michael Grant, *The History of Ancient Israel* (Scribner, 1984).

King Ahab of Israel

Israel sent 2,000 chariots and 10,000 soldiers to the battle, a deployment on a massive scale surpassed only by the 1,200 chariots, 1,200 horsemen, and 20,000 soldiers provided by Aram Damascus. Historians are unsure who actually won the conflict as no records from the eleven kingdoms exist and the Assyrians never directly acknowledged any victory or defeat in the area–which might actually be telling of a loss, since King Shalmaneser III did not like admitting to military failures. Shalmaneser III did successfully defeat at least 14,000 troops and captured numerous chariots and horses, but he did not return to the region for future military campaigns, which was yet another indicator that the Battle of Qarqar was either a draw or a loss for the Assyrians. King Ahab of Israel continued to rule until his death in 852 BCE around Gilead, where he was fighting for territory.

Aside from the Assyrians, another major enemy of the Israelites during Iron Age II was Moab. Moab existed before the kingdom of Israel and frequently clashed with the Israelites over the territory surrounding the Dead Sea and nearby freshwater rivers. Very little historical evidence remains of the state itself, but there are numerous records of battles fought over places like Galilee. Around 840 BCE, King Mesha of Moab ordered the inscription of the Mesha Stele, which celebrated a great victory over Israelite conquerors.

According to the actual script, the Moabites angered Chemosh, their deity, and he forced the people into Israelite subjugation as punishment. Not many records remain of this conflict, but it correlates with documents left behind by the Israelites, who lost territory around the 840s BCE. The Mesha Stele is additionally significant for possessing the first non-Semitic reference to the Israelite god Yahweh.

Israel's conflict with the Assyrians was not over. Around 738 BCE, the Assyrian king Tiglath-Pileser III occupied Philistia near Israel's border and swiftly invaded. The Israelites were vastly outnumbered and lacked the military technology possessed by the Neo-Assyrian Empire. Israel crumbled, the city of Samaria fell, and the former kingdom became a weakened vassal state forced to pay tribute to its conquerors. A vassal state was any political entity–often a kingdom– subordinate to another and often made to supplement the more powerful state's military and coffers. Thousands of Israelites were deported from their homes and sent to the borders where there were fewer resources, trade routes, and less arable farmland.

Judah

Judah's origins are unclear. Historians found evidence indicating that the region which would become the Kingdom of Judah had been inhabited for a long time by a separate group of Israelites, but there was no single center of power. Instead, these southern highlands were divided along separate familial or tribal lines throughout the 10th and 9th centuries BCE. Consolidation didn't begin until the reign of King Hezekiah, a notable Biblical figure with mounds of archaeological evidence to support what exactly happened during his rule[7]. Indeed, there are so many resources that some historians and archaeologists consider his disputes with the Assyrian Empire, to

---

[7] J. Maxwell Miller, *A History of Ancient Israel and Judah, Second Edition* (Louisville: Westminster John Knox Press, 2006).

whom Judah owed allegiance, to be the most well-documented events during the Iron Age.

King Hezekiah

Many historians look to the Old Testament of the Bible for a rough chronology of Hezekiah's life since numerous facts correlate with archaeological evidence discovered in the region. He was born around 739 BCE in the main city of Jerusalem and died around 687 BCE. King Hezekiah entered politics at the tender age of 10, when he served alongside his father Ahaz to learn the tricks of the trade. During his reign, literacy thrived and new literary works entered the public sphere, although these were accessible only to the wealthy or those in the administration. Jerusalem continued to serve as the population center of Judah and exploded into significance with its population increasing by a factor of five–it went from a sizable 5,000 citizens to a massive 25,000, which was huge for the Iron Age.[8]

The walls around Jerusalem received significant resizing and fortification to accommodate the new population, and Judah became one of the most powerful kingdoms along the Assyrian-Egyptian front. However, almost all of Judah's power and military

---

[8] The chronology of Judah's rise to power is confusing and confounded scholars for years. Under the rule of Hezekiah, Judah managed to gain power and consolidate before attempting to free itself from the Neo-Assyrian Empire. When the attempts failed and after Hezekiah perished, Judah appeared to embrace being a vassal state because the kingdom was afforded extra protection. However, chronological evidence is difficult to acquire.

concentrated on Jerusalem, where the majority of the population lived. This became a problem when Hezekiah denounced Assyrian dominance and rule, and the Assyrian king decided to march in with an army and take back the territory.

Records of the conflict between Judah and the Assyrians tell much of the same story. The Assyrian king Sennacherib heard about the rebellion of Judah and noticed several smaller states in the region additionally trying to escape Assyrian control. Sennacherib entered with an army and managed to reclaim numerous places, including Sidon and Ashkelon. Other states decided to pay tribute instead of fight, including the Moab mentioned earlier.

Afterward, Sennacherib marched his troops into Judah and conquered much of it but was forced to a standstill outside of Jerusalem. The newly-built walls defended the Judeans and the Assyrians laid siege to the massive capital for weeks. According to the Bible, an angel smote 185,000 Assyrian troops and Sennacherib retreated in defeat after receiving tribute from Hezekiah. Sennacherib instead wrote that the Assyrians sieged the city and left not because of losses, but because they received the tribute they wanted and a pledge that Judah would no longer rebel. Sennacherib's version of events can be found on the six-sided Prism of Nineveh, a stone statue that forms part of Sennacherib's Annals, or records.

King Hezekiah did eventually die, but not before performing one another major work which set the stage for the future of Judah. Hezekiah decided to completely overhaul and reform the Judean religion.[9] He purified the central temple in Jerusalem, reformed the priesthood, banned idols, and attacked the practice of idolatry, which was the worship of idols or statues believed to depict gods. Idols formed a major part of most of the ancient religions in the Levant, so the development of a group which did not use them was significant and would set the stage for the future practices of the Israelites, who

---

[9] Ibid.

did not depict the face or body of their deity like others did. Among the idols destroyed was the bronze serpent believed to have been made by Moses to cure others of snake bites.

Hezekiah's religious reforms occurred at a significant point in time during the history of the Israelites. Samaria of Israel had fallen and prophets appeared throughout Judah preaching that the same would happen to the Judean kingdom if it failed to reform religiously. To Hezekiah, Samaria's fall was tangible evidence that something needed to be done, especially with the Assyrians breathing down his neck. Besides the purging of idolatry, additional religious reforms included:

- The destruction of pagan home altars and the practice of polytheism by people who did not live in Jerusalem
- The centralization of religious practice in Jerusalem itself
- Granting power to the priests of Yahweh to destroy any pagan altars or artifacts they encountered
- The enforcement of pilgrimages to Jerusalem as a show of faith
- The celebration of Passover

Hezekiah's reforms didn't last long after his reign but continued to be significant to the developers of the Israelite religion. Shortly following the king's death, Judah embraced its role as a vassal state to the Assyrians to avoid being destroyed like nearby Israel and played a significant role in the development of the olive trade across the Levant. Judah prospered despite its subjugation and enjoyed immense wealth and power despite trying to free itself while Sennacherib was king. All of this changed when the Neo-Assyrian Empire came under attack by the Babylonians.

Chapter 4 – The Israelites under Babylon

The period before the disintegration of the Neo-Assyrian Empire could be considered a golden age for the Israelites. While Israel itself crumbled, Judah continued to thrive and might have remained prosperous for a long time if not for Assyria's infighting and inability to retain its territory. But who were the Babylonians, and what was their full effect on the lives of the Israelites?

Before the Neo-Babylonian Empire

To understand the fate of the Israelites, it's important to know just who the Neo-Babylonians were and what situation existed in Mesopotamia. The Empire emerged around 626 BCE and controlled vast quantities of the Levant until 539 BCE. For the three centuries prior to the empire's creation, the Babylonians were vassals to the far more powerful Assyrians, the same people who conquered Israel and controlled Judah. Indeed, the Babylonians might have remained under Assyrian control if not for the death of one of the most powerful Assyrian rulers in living memory: Ashurbanipal.

Tablet with Ashurbanipal

Ashurbanipal's death triggered an incredible amount of internal strife throughout the Neo-Assyrian Empire. He controlled the greatest expanse of territory ever owned by the Assyrians and, while beloved by his people, was known for his exceptional cruelty towards his enemies. Among the sadistic torments he inflicted upon his rivals was spiking a dog chain through the jaw of an enemy and forcing the man to live in a dog kennel until his death. Despite his violence, he was surprisingly lenient and even kind to his people, never massacring or committing such atrocities against them.

Ashurbanipal was also an extremely intelligent, learned man who strove to increase his empire's culture. As a child and young man, he underwent a thorough scribal education and was one of a few kings capable of reading the cuneiform script in Akkadian and Sumerian, two of the languages used in the region. He created the famous Library of Ashurbanipal, which contained over 30,000 tablets and texts from all around Mesopotamia–many were gathered during his conquests. He stored them in his library, which became the prototype for all future ones.

Upon his death in 627 BCE, Ashurbanipal was succeeded by his son, Ashur-etil-ilani. Ashur-etil-ilani only ruled for four years before a series of civil wars broke out. No clear records remain of what happened except that several members of the nobility vied for power. Assyria's enemies took advantage of the situation and hordes of Persians, Cimmerians, Scythians, Medes, and others descended upon the crumbling empire. They came down upon the empire like a wave, plundering, looting, and attacking towns and settlements as far south as Egypt. They could not capture the capital of Nineveh, but it was left weakened and the Neo-Assyrian Empire no longer exhibited control and influence over its former vassal states, including Judah.

The Neo-Babylonian Empire

Also called the Second Babylonian Empire, the Neo-Babylonian Empire originated around 626 BCE, when the Neo-Assyrian Empire faced collapse.[10] For the preceding three centuries, the Assyrians controlled Babylonia and treated it like a vassal state. Once the brutal civil wars following Ashurbanipal's death began, Babylonia sprang at the chance to free itself and create a powerful empire of its own. Alongside the Cimmerians, Scythians, and others, Babylonia sacked Nineveh in 612 BCE and started an empire which managed to control even more territory than that of the Assyrians. This map demonstrates the extent of the Neo-Babylonians at the height of their power.

---

[10] George Stephen Goodspeed, *A History of the Babylonians and Assyrians* (Independent Publishing, 2014).

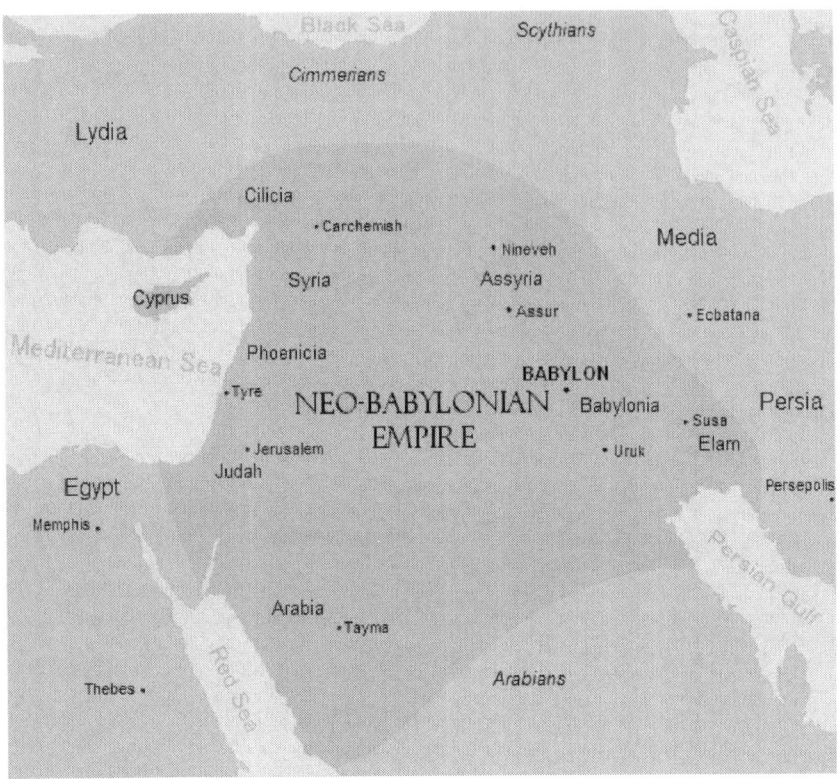

The Babylonians and a New Israelite Identity

When the Babylonians took over Assyrian territory they naturally claimed the former kingdom of Israel and the entirety of Judah. Whereas before Judah was prosperous and heavily involved in trade, it now became weak and disoriented. The kingdom entered a period of steep decline economically, and the population diminished from a combination of warfare and lower agricultural yields. A city in the northern half of Judah became the capital of a Babylonian province, while Jerusalem itself and its famous temple were destroyed following multiple rebellions. The entire infrastructure of the Judean capital completely collapsed, forcing many to wander away from their homes. This was a significant blow to the Israelites because their religion preached that Yahweh had selected Jerusalem as his permanent home and that they would hold the capital in perpetuity.

In particular, the exiled Israelites needed to come to terms with the idea that the original Davidic dynasty would no longer reign and the Israelites were not as infallible as believed. The majority of the people forced from Jerusalem were the elites, including princes, priests, prophets, scribes, and other administrators. Many stayed together and actually wrote or contributed to many of the sections of the Hebrew Bible, including the books of Ezekiel and Jeremiah. In the last quarter of the 20th and the beginning of the 21st century, scholars even discovered tablets written by the Israelite exiles describing their everyday lives in new settlements. Many of these Israelite refugees developed the religious doctrines of individualism and universalism, which dictated that a single god created people and the world.

Finally, perhaps the most influential aspect of this diaspora was the development of a distinct Hebrew identity for the Israelites which was used to separate them from other peoples in the area and around the world. It's important to note, though, that all of this literature neglects to state that the majority of the Israelites remained in Jerusalem under the rule of the Babylonians, and even experienced a better quality of life since they received most of the property taken from the elites.[11] Admittedly a few rebellions against the Babylonian governors existed, but mostly the Israelites who remained continued their lives in peace.

Outside of Jerusalem, the Israelites suffered. Similar to the Neo-Assyrian Empire, the Neo-Babylonians needed to conduct regular military campaigns throughout its territory just to maintain control. The Babylonians possessed too many enemies to fully manage their empire, and thus many of the Israelites outside of walled cities suffered raids and attacks from nearby peoples like the Arabs and Ammonites. Even worse, the Phoenicians conducted numerous slave

---

[11] Ranier Albertz, *Israel in Exile: The History and Literature of the Sixth Century B.C.E.*, (Society of Biblical Literature: 2003.)

raids in the areas to find people to sell in its trade routes along the Mediterranean Sea.

Rebellion and the Creation of Yehud

As briefly mentioned earlier, Jerusalem and its famous temple were only destroyed following two failed rebellions. The first occurred in the early 6th century, when the current king Zedekiah revolted against the Neo-Babylonian ruler, Nebuchadnezzar II. He entered into an alliance with the Egyptian pharaoh at the time but was unable to withstand the onslaught of the Babylonian military. When the Assyrians put down the rebellion around 597 BCE, numerous influential Israelites found themselves shipped to Babylon in captivity.

Judah decided to revolt again a few years later despite not gaining much military strength. In 589 BCE, the city of Jerusalem once again came under siege. After eighteen months, the city fell again the Babylonians and Nebuchadnezzar II. It was at this time that the city and the temple were razed and the entire administrative class of Jerusalem were banished or exiled to captivity in Babylon. Combined with the number of refugees who fled, archaeologists believe the kingdom of Judah lost 8,000 people, or roughly a quarter of the entire population.

Nebuchadnezzar II

With the elites removed and resistance thoroughly stamped out of the Israelites, Judah became a Babylonian province called Yehud. Nebuchadnezzar II originally appointed an Israelite to be his governor, a man named Gedaliah. Historians dispute what his exact role was and just how much autonomy he possessed; some say he truly was an administrative figure, while others think he was a puppet king taking orders from the Babylonian rulers. [12]

Originally, it seemed like Yehud and the Israelites who remained could live in peace. Many who fled the city during the rebellions returned when they heard a fellow Israelite and Judah native was in charge. However, someone assassinated Gedaliah and numerous rebels killed the Babylonian garrison defending and controlling the city. The Israelites in Yehud fled to Egypt to avoid Babylonian reprisals and Judah again descended into obscurity until the arrival of the Persians, who would wrest power from their Babylonian rivals.

---

[12] Ibid.

Chapter 5 – The Control of the Persians

As with all ancient empires, the Neo-Babylonians were incapable of holding on to all of the territory they captured from others. Although the Babylonians kept many of their enemies at bay, they were no match for a new threat: the Persians under Cyrus II, also known as Cyrus the Great. He created the largest empire ever seen in the world until that point in history: the Achaemenid Empire. It extended throughout the Middle East to Asia Minor, across the Mediterranean Sea to the future Greece, and into Northern Africa.

Cyrus the Great

Prior to the Persian invasion of the Neo-Babylonian Empire, Mesopotamia looked like this:

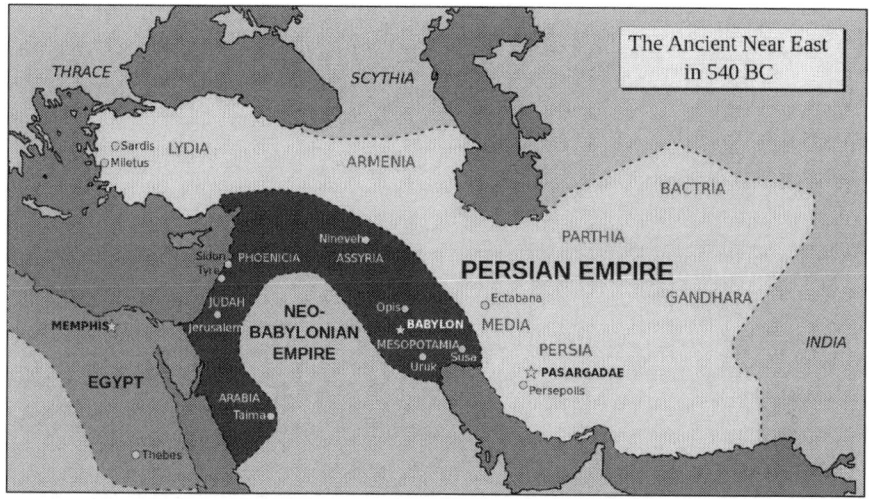

Judah was on the far western side of the Neo-Babylonian Empire, which demonstrates the sheer extent of Cyrus the Great's military power and prowess. He conquered several of his enemies in Asia Minor before turning his attention to the Babylonians. The deciding battle between the two powers is known as the Battle of Opis, which occurred around September and October of 539 BCE.

The Battle of Opis

Opis was a city along the river Tigris which served as a crucial entry point into the Neo-Babylonian Empire. Nebuchadnezzar II fully fortified the region during his reign and built a strong, gargantuan wall in an attempt to keep potential invaders away. This was called the Median Wall. Unfortunately for the Babylonians, one end of the wall was located in Opis. The city additionally featured a bridge which crossed the Mediterranean, making it a key place for the Persians to attempt their siege.

Not much is known about what actually happened during the battle. Instead, historians know that the Battle of Opis ended with a clear Persian victory and a total Babylonian defeat, if not an entire routing of the army. The Persians took a huge amount of plunder from the city and records indicate a massacre occurred, but no one knows if it was of the citizens of Opis or the retreating Babylonian army. Strangely, after this defeat, the Babylonians seemed to give up and allowed the Persians entry, possibly because Opis was made an example of. Other historians believe that Cyrus the Great actually made a deal with the Babylonian rulers after the destruction of their army which allowed the Persians to claim Opis peacefully.

The Israelites and the Persians

Once the Neo-Babylonian Empire crumbled, Yehud transformed into the autonomous province of Yehud Medinata. It was an important administrative zone but retained a small population of no more than 30,000 people at any given time. Once Cyrus the Great died, his successor managed to add Egypt to the Achaemenid Empire, a move which placed Yehud Medinata at the border of the empire and a troublesome frontier for the Persians. During the years of Persian control, some of the Israelites banished by the Babylonians returned to their homes but many stayed away.

After a period of turmoil following the Persian ruler's death in 522 BCE, Cyrus seized power in 521 BCE.[13] During his reign, he reformed the empire's administration and collected and codified the local laws throughout Persian territory. At this point, he decided to reform many of the law codes and how they were implemented throughout the region, resulting in the simultaneous redaction of the Torah and the suppression a huge portion of Israelite heritage. The Persians additionally transitioned the region from speaking Hebrew on a daily basis to Aramaic, although Hebrew continued to be used for religious purposes. Despite these changes, Cyrus is known in the Christian Bible as being a liberator of Judah, potentially because he defeated the original Babylonian conquerors.

---

[13] Matt Waters, *Ancient Persia: A Concise History of the Achaemenid Empire, 550-330 BCE* (New York: Cambridge University Press, 2014).

Eventually, the population of Yehud Medinata managed to rebuild Jerusalem and its temple, but the city's population never exceeded 1,500 people. The city once again became the capital, this time of the Persian province in the Achaemenid Empire. Historians suspect that the Persian government initially tried to set up a kingdom to manage the province, most likely run by the descendants of Jehoiachin. Jehoiachin was the king of Judah before it fell to the Babylonians. Around the mid-5th century though, Yehud Medinata and especially the city of Jerusalem became run by a theocracy with hereditary high priests. A governor appointed by the Persians, almost always a Jewish man, collected taxes and kept the order within the province.

The province of Yehud Medinata was significantly smaller than the old kingdom of Judah. The majority of the people lived in tiny towns without walls and either worked as farmers or shepherds. The Persians used the province as a military outpost since it was along the border of their empire and set up a couple of minting facilities for coins since there were nearby resources and mines.[14] Although the Old Testament claims over 43,000 exiled Israelites returned to the region, evidence indicates that the population actually declined at this time. At certain points, there were as few as 500 people in the capital of Jerusalem.

Persian Influence on Language, Literature, and Religion

As briefly mentioned in the last section, the language of the Israelites shifted from Hebrew to Aramaic. Aramaic belongs to the same Semitic subfamily as Hebrew and possesses many similarities. In particular, both languages were written using the Hebrew alphabet and Aramaic itself, at least in the region of Yehud, contained numerous Hebrew words, prefixes, and suffixes. Some scholars

---

[14] Ibid.

believe the two languages to be as close to one another as Spanish and Portuguese are in contemporary times. Aramaic seems to have arrived with the Persian Empire, where many of the members spoke the language.

There were also changes in literature, particularly the final forms of the Torah or Biblical Old Testament. Some of the ancient books originally included in religious practices disappeared and were replaced with new writings. Among these creations were Ben Sira, Tobit, Judith, Enoch 1, and Maccabees. The books from Joshua to Kings underwent enormous revision and editing to develop their complete forms as well. The writing additionally became more authoritative, hinting at the development of a body of scripture designed to tell the official story of religion and people's practices.

Along with these developments in the holy work of the Israelites came changes in actual religious practice and thought. During the 9th and 8th centuries BCE, the Israelites weren't fully monotheistic. There still existed the worship of family gods and fertility cults, and not even the input of the Assyrians, who believed their king to be divine, hurried the process of the Israelite deity becoming singular. This changed around the arrival of the Persians, who brought the influence of Zoroastrianism.

Zoroastrianism is one of the oldest known religions in human existence. It preaches the existence of a supreme being who created the universe, a clear dichotomy between good and evil, and an eschatology which predicts the fall of evil and the end of human history.[15] Some believe that Zoroastrianism influenced the Israelites to fully adopt the idea of a supreme, powerful Yahweh and the movement of other ancestral gods to becoming angels and demons in a separate pantheon. It would be surprising if Zoroastrianism and the Persians didn't have any influence on the Israelite religion considering the Persians controlled almost the entire population for

---

[15] An eschatology is a theology which predicts the end of human events or the ultimate destiny of humanity – most modern religions have one.

over a century, and similar influences can be found in other dominated areas.

The Persian Achaemenid Empire

A final development for the Israelites was the cemented idea of "otherness," which started with the exiles during the Babylonian occupation and gradually spread throughout Yehud. Previously, the Israelites possessed cordial relationships with their neighboring peoples and intermarriage occurred frequently even if it was not wholly supported. During the Persian dominance over the Israelites, the exiles who returned to Jerusalem and the former Judah started to spread the idea of being the chosen people of Yahweh, who was now a supreme being. Because they were chosen, the Israelites could not marry non-members of the religion without losing that status.

The Fall of the Achaemenid Empire in the Levant

The former kingdoms of Israel and Judah once again saw turmoil and conflict beginning in the 4th century BCE when the Achaemenid Empire came under attack by one of history's most discussed figures–Alexander the Great. Alexander the Great, whose real name was Alexander III of Macedon, hailed from an ancient Greek kingdom. He succeeded his father at the tender age of 20 and immediately began military campaigns that spanned Europe, Asia, and Africa. After two years on the throne, Alexander implemented his late father's plans to expand into Persian territory and started to wage war in 334 BCE.[16]

Alexander the Great

Despite bordering the Mediterranean Sea, Yehud remained untouched by the early invasion. Alexander chose to attack the Achaemenid Empire through Anatolia, which forms modern-day Turkey. The ruler of the Persians at the time, a man named Darius III, did not believe Alexander, who led the Greek Hellenic League, would be able to claim territory and so he remained in the capitol of Persepolis. His plan was for the satraps, or governors, of the Anatolian provinces to handle the problem with their own militaries. When that failed and Alexander gained ground quickly, Darius III

---

[16] Professor Thomas R. Martin and Christopher W. Blackwell, *Alexander the Great: The Story of an Ancient Life* (New York: Cambridge University Press, 2012).

left Persepolis and set out with his own forces to meet the Greek general on the battlefield.

Leading the Persians, Darius III suffered a humiliating and devastating defeat during the Battle of Issus, which took place near the modern town of Issus in Turkey. Despite appearing with over twice the number of troops and cavalry, Darius III was routed by Alexander and lost his hold over Anatolia. Even more embarrassing was that Alexander abducted Darius III's wife, daughters, and mother, since they had accompanied the Persian king on his campaign. The Battle of Issus occurred in 333 BCE and marked the beginning of the Achaemenid Empire's end.

Albrecht Altdorfer's Battle of Alexander at Issus

At this point, Darius III offered Alexander a peace treaty where Alexander could keep the conquered territory and be given 10,000 talents in exchange for the Persian king's family. Alexander refused, claiming he was now the king of Asia. Later in 333 BCE, he marched down into the Levant, in which lay the province of Yehud. The entire area resisted and Alexander made an example of the city of Tyre, in modern Lebanon. After a long siege of many months, Tyre fell and Alexander had all men of military age executed, while the women and children were sold into slavery. The rest of the region fell quickly with little resistance, including Yehud.

The Israelites under Alexander the Great

Alexander did little in the way of administration or actual ruling. He collected tribute in a manner similar to the Persians and had no problem allowing captured peoples to continue to practice their culture and religion, which allowed the Israelites to continue their worship of Yahweh. While his conquest did promote Hellenization, or the spread of the Greek language and incorporation of cultural elements into other societies, this wasn't really seen with the Israelites.

Instead, fates wouldn't change for the Israelites until Alexander the Great died shortly after beginning his conquests around 323 BCE, at the age of 32.[17] This was a problem because the conqueror did not have a clear successor. His son was born after his death, and although his bodyguard and one of the leading generals chose to be joint kings until the child was old enough to assume the throne, it all fell apart. The generals chosen to lead individual satrapies began to fight amongst themselves, spawning a conflict that would last for 40 years. Eventually, Alexander's Empire became split into four separate parts: Ptolemaic Egypt, Seleucid Mesopotamia and Central Asia, Attalid Anatolia, and Antigonid Macedon. The Israelites belonged to Seleucid Mesopotamia and Central Asia.

---

[17] Ibid.

Chapter 6 – The Hellenistic Period and Judea under the Seleucids

While the Israelites would eventually become part of Seleucid Mesopotamia and Central Asia, this didn't happen immediately. During the infighting between Alexander's generals, the province of Yehud came under the control of a man known as Ptolemy I, from whose name the term "Ptolemaic Egypt" is derived. In 321 BCE, Alexander's bodyguard and friend Perdiccas tried to invade Egypt. He lost a major battle at the Nile River, and his own men murdered him that night while he slept in his tent. Ptolemy I was Perdiccas' enemy and the satrap of Egypt. Once Perdiccas failed to take the area, his men defected to Ptolemy's army.

Ptolemy I

Ptolemy I was an intriguing figure. According to his claimed ancestry, he was the half-brother of Alexander, a fact that preserved genealogical records state might be the truth. Unlike many of the other generals of Alexander who overstepped their own abilities with their lust for power, Ptolemy I possessed a solid strategy that started at home. Although he had expansionist dreams, he knew he could never retake the entirety of Alexander's conquests and turned his attention to securing Egypt before moving to the surrounding region. In particular, he desired Cyrenaica, Cyprus, and Syria, including the new province of Judea–Judah once again.[18]

Over two decades, Ptolemy claimed and then evacuated Syria four times because of the fighting between Alexander's generals. The third and fourth times occurred around 302 and 301 BCE. Ptolemy I joined a coalition to oust an especially powerful general gaining territory, and he occupied Syria along the battlefront. However, he received some wrong information and, thinking his friends were defeated, he left. When he discovered the error, he returned, but it was too late. The coalition believed he deserted them and thus gave away Syria and Judea to Seleucus I Nicator, the satrap of Babylon.

Due to his thirst for power, excellent military strategy, and sheer determination, Seleucus managed to claim the entire eastern section of Alexander's empire, which included Asia and Anatolia. However, like many of the other generals, Seleucus grew greedy and attempted to take several of the European territories held by others, including Thrace and Macedon. He arrived in Thrace in 281 BCE and was assassinated by some rivals hiding in the court. His son, Antiochus I, replaced him, and the Israelites continued under the powerful Seleucid Empire.

---

[18] Ian Worthington, *Ptolemy I: King and Pharaoh of Egypt* (New York: Oxford University Press, 2016).

Seleucus as Depicted on a Coin

Hellenization and Antiochus IV

In general, the Israelites did not object to living under the control of the Seleucid Empire so long as they remained capable of practicing their religion, now referred to as Judaism. However, this does not mean they agreed with one another over how life should be. As mentioned earlier, Alexander brought with him a period of Hellenization, where Greek culture, ideas, and even language began to spread across Europe, Asia, and Africa. Some Israelites favored the process of Hellenization, while others vehemently opposed it. Many people also could not agree whether or not Judea should be loyal to the dynasty of the Ptolemies or Seleucids, since they had lived over one or the other all within a few decades.

These tensions came to a head in 175 BCE, when the High Priest Simon II died.[19] He had two sons who could inherit his position. The first was Onias III, who favored the Ptolemies and opposed Hellenization. The second was Jason, who supported the Seleucids as well as the process of Hellenization. What followed was not well-documented, but it is known that years of political and court intrigue developed, during which multiple people tried to bribe the king for the position of High Priest. Accusations of murder clogged the air between contenders. Eventually, a minor civil war broke out.

---

[19] The High Priest at this time would be the chief religious official for the entire province, whose ecclesiastical authority was only outmatched by the king.

At the end, Jason ascended to the position of High Priest and began Hellenization by erecting an arena for games and a gymnasium near the Jewish temple in Jerusalem. Some people even underwent the process of non-surgical foreskin restoration so they could associate naked with others in the gym–as was the Greek custom–without ridicule.

The next problem for the Israelites came from the rule of Antiochus IV Epiphanes. He was a Seleucid king from 175 BCE-164 BCE. During his reign, he launched an attack against Egypt, supposedly without any Jewish support. When he was forced to return by Rome, he and his men stopped in Jerusalem and sacked the temple, stealing important religious idols and treasures. The soldiers additionally massacred an unknown number of Jews. Shortly after the assault, Antiochus IV imposed harsh laws in Judea that attempted to cripple the Israelites' religion. Among them were forbidding the possession of Jewish scriptures, the practice of circumcision, and trying to enforce the worship of Zeus. These attacks against the Jewish religion can be seen in the religious book of Maccabees, which says:

"And after that Antiochus had smitten Egypt, he returned again in the hundred forty and third year, and went up against Israel

and Jerusalem with a great multitude,

And entered proudly into the sanctuary, and took away the golden altar, and the candlestick of light, and all the vessels thereof...

And when he had taken all away, he went into his own land, having made a great massacre, and spoken very proudly.

Therefore there was a great mourning in Israel, in every place where they were."[20]

---

[20] 1 Maccabees 20:25.

Antiochus IV

Antiochus IV's actions did not go undisputed. Numerous members of the Judean population revolted against Seleucid rule in an event known as the Maccabean Revolt.

Maccabean Revolt

Although religious books depict the Maccabean Revolt as a full rebellion against the Seleucids, many modern scholars believe it was actually part of a civil war between those Israelites who wished to be Hellenized and those who refused. According to the literature, the revolt began when a rural Jewish priest named Mattathias the Hasmonean refused to worship the Greek gods and then killed another man who tried to place an offering to an idol in the town. He and his five sons fled into the wilderness, where Mattathias died roughly one year later.

1866 Painting by Gustave Doré of Mattathias

Once Mattathias died, his son Judah led an army of dissidents out of the wilderness in 166 BCE. The dissidents fought against the Seleucids through guerilla warfare and actions which would be questionable today. Along the way, they destroyed pagan altars, forcibly circumcised young boys, and attacked Hellenized Jews. The warfare occurred primarily through a series of small battles where the quick, lightning tactics of the light Maccabee infantry frequently triumphed over the slower Seleucids. The main known conflicts include:

- Battle of Wadi Haramia (167 BCE)
- Battle of Beth Horon (166 BCE)
- Battle of Emmaus (166 BCE)
- Battle of Beth Zur (164 BCE)
- Battle of Beth Zechariah (162 BCE)
- Battle of Adasa (161 BCE)

- Battle of Elasa (160 BCE)

Eventually, the Maccabee forces triumphed and entered Jerusalem. They cleansed and rededicated the temple while reestablishing traditional Jewish worship. At the same time, they named Jonathan Maccabee as the High Priest. The Seleucid Empire did send a battalion of soldiers to retake Jerusalem, but they ultimately retreated when Antiochus IV died shortly thereafter.

Chapter 7 – The Early Hasmonean Dynasty

Judea slowly entered a new period under the control of the Hasmonean Dynasty. This dynasty consisted of Matthias and his sons, who claimed Judea and parts of the surrounding territory. During its initial years, the Hasmonean Dynasty served as a vassal state for the weakening Seleucid Empire but would eventually gain some autonomy before succumbing to the Romans to the west.

Matthias' son Judah led the majority of the conflict against the Seleucids. The Judeans possessed several military advantages because the majority of the battles were fought on Judean home territory and featured fast, guerrilla units against the slower, more established Seleucids. However, the Maccabees that formed the Hasmonean Dynasty might never have seen victory if not for internal conflicts within the Seleucid Empire caused by disputes over power and poor foreign relationships with nearby powers like Ptolemaic Egypt.

Demetrius I Soter was the primary enemy of Judah and the one who possessed weaknesses to be exploited, but only after Judah's death. As mentioned previously, Judah led most of the military conflicts on behalf of the Maccabees and thus saw the most combat during the rise of the Hasmonean Dynasty. He came face to face on the battlefield with Demetrius I Soter's generals multiple times, including at the infamous Battle of Elasa.

While Demetrius I Soter was handling affairs to the east, he sent a man by the name of Bacchides to handle his territory's affairs to the west. Bacchides chose to attack the rising autonomous power of Judea under the Maccabees and received Demetrius I Soter's approval to begin offensive military actions. During the battle of Elasa, he marched upon Jerusalem with over 20,000 men, including heavily armed infantry arranged in a classical phalanx formation. Judah only had 3,000 men protecting Jerusalem along with himself, and sources indicate at least 2/3 of the army fled upon seeing the Seleucid forces. After a tense struggle between the Seleucids and remaining Maccabee forces, Judah was executed and the territory once more taken over by the Seleucid Empire.

Death of Judas Maccabeus by José Teófilo de Jesus

Bacchides established a new order in Jerusalem with the Hellenes in charge of the region of Israel. Jonathan, a brother of Judah, took the remaining patriots who didn't die during the conflict and escaped across the Jordan River. They engaged in several military battles and eventually stayed in hiding in the swamps of the area. Bacchides decided to leave Israel. However, less than two years later, a city called Acre faced a significant enough threat from the remaining

Maccabees that they contacted Demetrius I Soter for assistance. He sent Bacchides back to the area.

Jonathan and his forces were more experienced in guerrilla warfare than before and met Bacchides in the desert before retreating to a fortress called Beth-hogla. Bacchides lay siege to Jonathan's hideout for several days. Afterward, sources are unclear. The Books of the Maccabees indicate that Jonathan entered into a peace treaty with Bacchides, where they exchanged hostages and declared an end to hostilities. The books then say that Bacchides left and never returned, while Jonathan kept up the fight to establish a new dynasty.

Alexander Balas

What is known is that Demetrius I Soter was struggling due to poor international relationships with nearby leaders. Among the many people who denounced him or chose to stop cooperating with him were several other rulers who chose to stop acknowledging Demetrius I Soter as the legitimate ruler of the Seleucids. Instead, people like Ptolemy VI and Cleopatra of Egypt and Attalus II Philadelphus of Pergamon supported Alexander Balas, who pushed forward his own claim to the throne.

Coin with Profile of Alexander Balas

Alexander Balas actually had no legitimate claim to the throne. He came from the city of Smyrna and was a commoner, but he pretended to be the child of Antiochus IV Epiphanes and Laodice

IV. Heracleides, a former minister and eventual usurper of power, discovered Alexander Balas and his sister and started pushing them forth as the legitimate children of the dead king and queen. Despite being executed by Demetrius I Soter, Heracleides' claims stuck and Alexander Balas received recognition from the Roman Senate and the Ptolemaic Dynasty of Egypt.

Alexander Balas moved against Demetrius I Soter in the 150s BCE. He allied himself with the Maccabees by suggesting a counteroffer to Jonathan which beat out Demetrius I Soter's promises of legitimacy and free rule of Judea. Alexander Balas promised that Jonathan could become the new, uncontested high priest and recruit his own army to defend Jerusalem. Jonathan waited for Demetrius I Soter to recall his garrisons from Judea and listened as the current ruler of the Seleucid Empire promised him some autonomous rule. He moved to Jerusalem in 153 BCE, gradually amassed an army, and built his own garrisons. When war broke out, Jonathan–and by extension, the Israelites–all sided with Alexander Balas. Alexander Balas trounced Demetrius I Soter in 150 BCE.

Afterward, he extended an invitation to Jonathan. The new High Priest of Jerusalem could attend the new Seleucid emperor's wedding to a princess of the Ptolemaic Dynasty and was allowed to sit at the high table as an honored guest. Alexander Balas even briefly allowed Jonathan to wear the royal robe and graciously accepted the Israelite's gifts and praise. Jonathan was now the autonomous ruler of Judea and spurred forward the Hasmonean Dynasty. Alexander Balas appointed him as the military general and provincial governor of Judea under Seleucid protection and ignored complaints from the Hellenistic party in favor of his war ally.

Jonathan's Rule

Alexander Balas' time as ruler was short. In 147 BCE, a man named Demetrius II Nicator challenged Balas. Demetrius II Nicator was a son of Demetrius I Soter and started a lengthy war with Balas. While the seat of the Seleucid Empire was in disarray, the governor of the entirety of Coele-Syria challenged Jonathan. Judea existed within this larger province, and Governor Apollonius Taos decided to use the chaos of the monarchy to drive the Jews away from Jerusalem. [21]

The Location of Coele-Syria

Jonathan met Apollonius Taos on the battlefield with 10,000 soldiers. They marched to the city of Jaffa and attacked rapidly, forcing the unprepared city to open its gates. Apollonius called for reinforcements to defend Jaffa and received them from the separate city of Azotus. He challenged Jonathan on the battlefield and appeared with 3,000 infantry troops, including a powerful cavalry. Despite this advantage, Jonathan managed to route Apollonius. He captured and burned Azotus for its part in the attack and destroyed the internal temple of Dagon, an ancient fertility god. Alexander

---

[21] Igor P. Lipovsky, *Judea Between Two Eras* (Boston: Cambridge Publishing, Inc., 2017).

Balas rewarded Jonathan with the city of Ekron and its surrounding territory, and Jonathan returned in peace to Jerusalem.

The battle between Alexander Balas and Demetrius II Nicator waged on. On Demetrius II's side was his father-in-law, Ptolemy VI. Ptolemy VI met Alexander Balas on the field during the Battle of Antioch in 145 BCE. Alexander Balas lost his life and so did Ptolemy VI. Demetrius II managed to become the sole ruler of the Seleucid Empire and married the dead Balas' wife to further solidify his legitimacy.

Jonathan was not loyal to the new king and instead amassed his forces to lay siege to the Acra. The Acra was a prominent Seleucid fortress in Jerusalem and symbolized the empire's power over Judea. At the time, it was one of the most heavily fortified sections of the city and served as a shelter for Judean Hellenists who wished to exist under the control of the Seleucids. Jonathan's attack did not succeed. Demetrius II himself appeared at the nearby city of Ptolemais with a grand army and demanded to see Jonathan in person to hold him accountable for his betrayal.

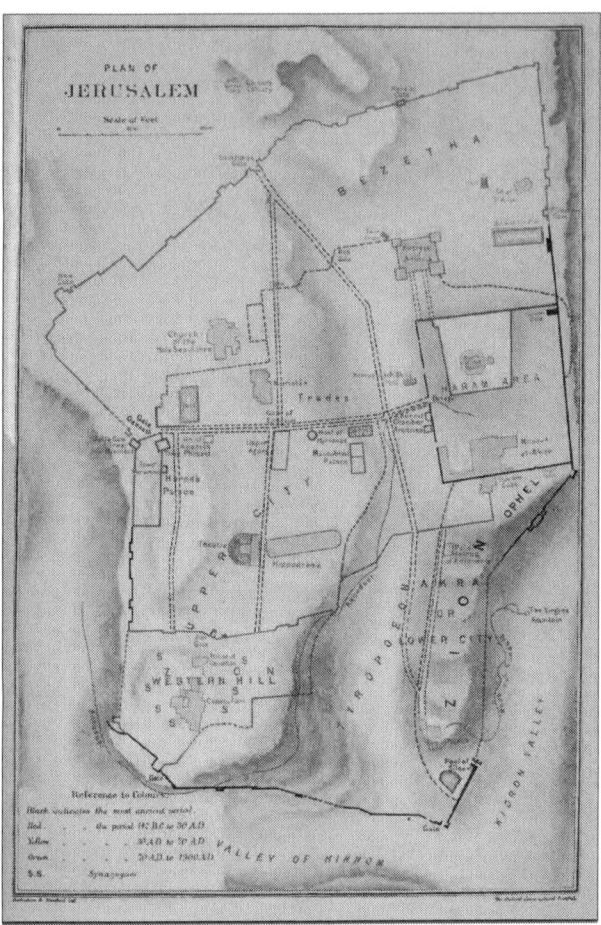

1903 Map of Jerusalem with the Acra

Jonathan appeared before Demetrius II and bought the emperor's favor with presents and gifts. Demetrius II acknowledged Jonathan's position as High Priest and seemed to forgive the attack on the Acra on the condition that Jonathan calls off the siege and never attempt a similar act in the future. Demetrius II additionally accepted the large sum of 300 talents from Jonathan, exempted Judea from taxes for a short period of time, and granted the High Priest the nearby toparchies (an area to be governed) of Mount Ephraim, Lod, and Ramathaim-Zophim.[22]

Again, peace would not last. Demetrius II soon found himself challenged by a man named Diodotus Tryphon, a former general of Alexander Balas. He served as the tutor and caretaker of Balas' surviving three-year-old son, who Diodotus intended to use as a puppet ruler while he became king instead. Demetrius II promised to withdraw his battalions from the city of Acre in Jerusalem in exchange for the loyalty of Jonathan. He also wanted troops from Judea since his own forces were stretched thin from uprisings throughout the empire; many people supported Diodotus.

Jonathan sent roughly 3,000 troops to Demetrius II. They protected the king in his own city from the subjects of the Seleucid Empire. However, Demetrius II did not remove the garrisons like he promised, and Jonathan decided to defect in the manner of any other loyal, annoyed subject. Diodotus rewarded Jonathan's support by reaffirming his position as High Priest and appointing Jonathan's brother, Simon, as the military general in charge of the sea coast and part of the territory leading from Judea to Egypt.

Jonathan and Simon then went on a series of military conquests and started reaffirming their treaties with realms like the Roman Republic. However, Jonathan overreached himself. His aspirations to power did not go unnoticed, and Diodotus invited the High Priest to meet with him. Diodotus arrived outside of Judea with an army and awaited Jonathan in the city of Scythopolis. Jonathan arrived with 1,000 men, believing he would be given additional fortresses to control. Diodotus instead slaughtered Jonathan's soldiers and took the High Priest prisoner for his actions.

---

[22] A Roman talent equaled roughly 32.3 kilograms of a precious metal, so a significant amount of gold.

The Leadership of Simon

Diodotus attempted to invade Judea but ran straight into Jonathan's brother, Simon. Diodotus tried to talk Simon into peace by promising to release Jonathan in exchange for 100 talents of gold and substituting Jonathan's two sons as hostages. Simon reluctantly agreed because he didn't want to cause the death of his brother, but he didn't trust Diodotus in the least. Sure enough, Diodotus had Jonathan executed after receiving the money and hostages.

Simon became the official leader and High Priest of Judea in 142 BCE. The entirety of the Judean priests and nobility established a resolution to keep the Hasmoneans in power until a prophet appeared who would then lead the people. Considering how hard the Maccabees fought against Hellenization, it is ironic to note that this resolution, from which they would benefit, was established in the Hellenic fashion.[23]

Under Simon, the Hasmonean Dynasty would truly begin. He finally captured the Seleucid citadel in Jerusalem around 141 BCE. By 139 BCE, Rome recognized the Dynasty during Simon's visit. Judea seemed capable of running itself and holding off future incursions from the Seleucid Empire for a short amount of time. Simon ruled in peace from 142 BCE until 135 BCE, when he was abruptly assassinated. His killer was none other than his own son-in-law, who additionally murdered Simon's two oldest sons in an attempt to become closer to the throne.[24]

---

[23] Ibid.
[24] J.W. Rogerson, *The Oxford Handbook of Biblical Studies*, (OUP Oxford: 2006), p. 292.

Simon of the Maccabees

Chapter 8 – The Hasmonean Expansion and Civil War

John Hyrcanus

John Hyrcanus came to the throne as the third oldest son of Simon. He assumed leadership and accepted the title of High Priest while also taking a Hellenized name to appease certain members of the Seleucid Empire. Upon his accession to the throne, Hyrcanus was 30 years old and Judea and the Seleucid Empire were once again teetering on the precipice of war. Sure enough, the Seleucid king Antiochus VII Sidetes attacked Jerusalem.

Antiochus VII burned and pillaged the countryside around Jerusalem before laying siege to the city for an entire year. Hyrcanus chose to evacuate every citizen within the city who was unable to assist with the defense of Jerusalem. Naturally, Antiochus VII refused to let the refugees pass beyond his front lines. The refugees were therefore stuck between the two sides of the siege and suffered from starvation, abuse from the soldiers, and various illnesses common on the battlefield. Hyrcanus eventually came to his senses and allowed the refugees back in, but faced increased food shortages and starvation in Jerusalem. Once one year passed, he tried to negotiate a settlement with Antiochus VII.

Coin of John Hyrcanus

Antiochus VII agreed to a truce. Together, he and Hyrcanus mapped out a treaty which pleased the Seleucid Empire and stole power from Judea. In exchange for peace, Hyrcanus paid Antiochus VII 3,000 talents of silver which he was supposedly forced to remove from the tomb of the famous King David. He additionally needed to tear down the protective walls of Jerusalem, participate in the Seleucid war against their enemy the Parthians, and recognize Seleucid control of Judea. Together, all of these terms were extremely harsh and designed to weaken and break the power the Hasmonean Dynasty had built over the years.

Judea suffered economically following the war, in no small part because the Seleucid Empire decided to impose heavy taxes on the region. Hyrcanus left his position to accompany Antiochus VII during his military campaign against the Parthians, where he was made to lead Jewish forces.[25] He quickly lost support among the Judean population because of his absence and inexperience in politics. The people in the countryside hated him for allowing the Seleucids to plunder their lands, while religious folks loathed him for looting the tomb of David to retrieve the talents of silver. At the tender age of 31, Hyrcanus was hated by his own people.

This would all change following the death of Antiochus VII in 128 BCE, who was killed in the battle against the Parthians. Hyrcanus

---

[25] Joseph Sievers, and Jacob Neusner, ed., *The Hasmoneans and Their Supporters: From Matthias to the Death of John Hyrcanus I.* (Atlanta.: Scholars Press, 1990), 140.

recognized his advantage and manipulated the unrest in the Seleucid Empire following its loss of a leader. Demetrius II returned from exile to try and regain control of the entire empire, but was unable to make headway against the empowered Judea. Even worse, the Seleucid Empire found itself disintegrating into separate principalities since the princes could not agree who should control the territory. These new principalities included the Ammonites of the Transjordan, the Ituraeans of Lebanon, and the Arabian Nabateans, all of whom lived near Judea, the future Hasmonean Kingdom.[26]

John Hyrcanus began to carry out military campaigns to conquer former Seleucid territory around 113 BCE. The first target on his list was Samaria, a land in the location of contemporary Palestine and close to Judea. He began an extensive and exhausting military campaign to weaken Samaria's defenses and placed his sons in charge of the siege. Samaria knew it would be difficult to defeat the army Hyrcanus developed in the Seleucid Empire's absence and called for help. One of the kings of the Seleucid Empire sent 6,000 troops.[27]

Hyrcanus continued the siege for a year until the entire region crumbled. The mercenaries of the Seleucid king met their deaths, and Hyrcanus began a policy of forcing non-Jews to start practicing Jewish customs and laws. Many of the inhabitants of Samaria found themselves enslaved to the Judeans, and soon the city of Scythopolis fell as well.

The ambitions of Hyrcanus continued unabated. He next placed his sights on the Transjordan in 110 BCE. The Transjordan was the southern Levant east of the Jordan River and east of Judea. Hyrcanus first attacked the city of Medeba and claimed it as his own within six months. He next captured Shechem and Mount Gerizim, where he destroyed Samaritan temples and religious relics in order to spread

---

[26] Gaalyahu Cornfled, *Daniel to Paul: Jews In Conflict with Graeco-Roman Civilization*, (New York: The Macmillan Company, 1962), 50.
[27] Lipovsky, *Judea between Two Eras*.

Judaism. His attacks upon so-called pagan gods and religious idols raised his reputation among his people, especially the religious conservatives who were angry about the opening of David's tomb. Indeed, Hyrcanus's continued military successes greatly improved his worth in the eyes of the Israelites since it seemed they were coming to power again in the region.

Hyrcanus then chose to go south and attack the Edomites who lived south of Judea. He conquered numerous towns and then mandated the peoples undergo forced conversions to Judaism, a move unseen in any previous Judean ruler. Some sources say the people converted willingly to keep living in their territory, but others indicate that the Edomites were forced to undergo circumcisions and practice Jewish law under the threat of death.

Aside from his military accomplishments, Hyrcanus was well-known for his stabilization of Judea's position in the Levant. The siege of Jerusalem left Judea in dire financial straits, a problem which was solved by conquest. Places like Samaria now paid tribute to Judea, and Hyrcanus was able to issue his own coinage and start several building projects, including the creation of the fortress Hyrcania in the desert. He additionally made peace treaties with growing powers like the Roman Republic, the Greek kingdoms of Athens and Pergamum, and even Ptolemaic Egypt.

The Successors of John Hyrcanus

Peace would not last though. When Hyrcanus died, he decreed that his wife should become the new ruler, with the eldest of his five sons becoming the High Priest rather than the next king. The eldest son, Aristobulus I, did not take the news well. When his father died, he imprisoned his mother and three of his brothers. He allowed his mother to starve to death while he took the throne, only to die from an excruciating illness less than one year later, in 103 BCE.

Aristobulus I

During his short reign, Aristobulus I expanded his father's conquests even further. He claimed Galilee, a region in modern northern Israel. Despite resistance from local tribes and difficult terrain, the Judeans easily marched through Galilee and forced the native peoples to convert to Judaism. The practice of forced circumcision was especially common in the region.

Upon his death, Aristobulus I's wife, Salome Alexandra, released his brothers from prison. She chose to place Alexander Jannaeus on the throne and married him to keep her position. Alexander reigned from 103 BCE-76 BCE, during which he fought a long civil war against the Seleucid king Demetrius III Eucaerus. He additionally dealt with internal rebellions in Jerusalem and crucified over 800 Jewish rebels in a display of force.

The Hasmonean Dynasty lost its control of the Transjordan around 93 BCE to an Arab people from the southern Levant, and Alexander found himself forced to pay off his enemies so they wouldn't side with revolutionaries in Jerusalem who wanted him removed from power. Alexander died around 76 BCE and was replaced by Salome Alexandra, who ruled from 76 BCE-67 BCE. She was one of only two Jewish queens. She appointed her son to be her High Priest, and he would become the new king upon her death. During her reign, the Hasmonean Kingdom stretched to its largest extent.

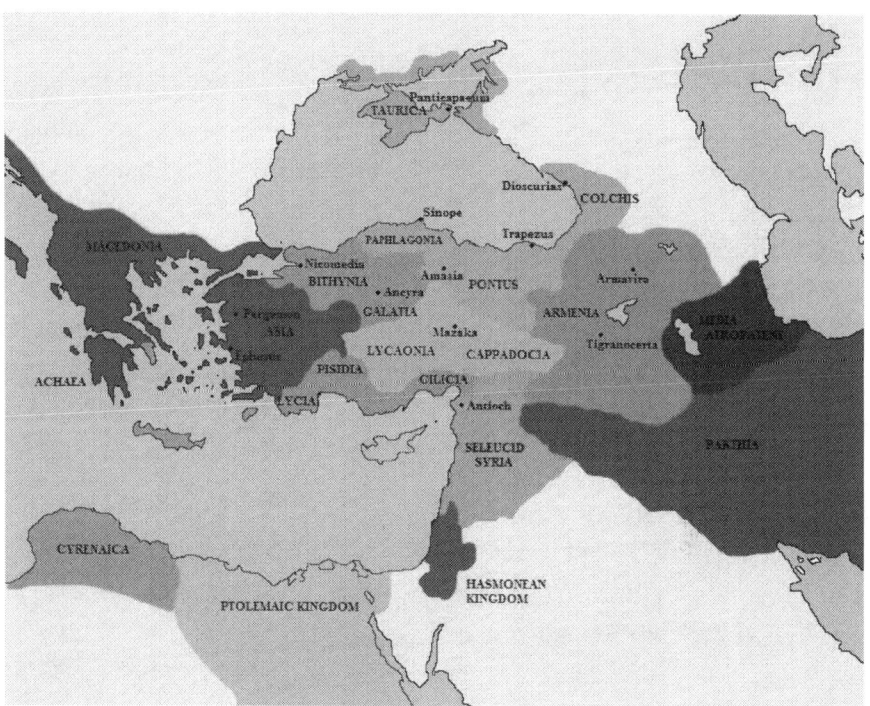

The Hasmonean Kingdom

The Pharisees and Sadducees

The Hasmonean Dynasty contended with two separate political and religious factions during its existence: the Pharisees and the Sadducees. The Pharisees as a party emerged shortly after John Hyrcanus established his new monarchy and developed an Israelite dynasty not based around the familial lines of David, as seen previously. The word "Pharisees" roughly translates to "separatists" and referred to a group of Israelites who observed traditional purity laws and maintained the old representation of the Torah, the law of God as spoken to Moses. The Pharisees' main base consisted of the lower classes and common peoples.

Most Sadducees were upper-class individuals who controlled the political and social aspects of Judea. The Sadducees ignored the oral tradition of the Torah, which the Pharisees followed. They adopted a more literal translation of the holy documents as well, which many viewed as continued Hellenization of traditional Jewish beliefs.

The Pharisees and Sadducees separated the classes and eventually formed the political factions which would become the sides of the Hasmonean Civil War. The Pharisees supported the old way of Jewish life and opposed many of the actions of the Hasmonean Dynasty, including the wars of expansion and forced conversions. The separation between the two parties grew even worse when the Pharisees demanded that Alexander Jannaeus choose between being High Priest or king. In response, Jannaeus implemented the rites of the Sadducees at the central Israelite Temple.[28]

A brief riot broke out in the Temple, as the Pharisees angrily attacked the king's decision. It was quickly put down and a period of stringent persecution of the Pharisees began. When Jannaeus died, he begged the two sides to reconcile their differences, but this was unlikely. Salome Alexandra took over and her brother was an important Pharisee, which put them temporarily in power. When she died, her two sons, each boasting a claim to the throne, sided with separate factions to gain support. The competing power bases which resulted would back the two claimants through a bloody period of civil war.

Hasmonean Civil War

Hyrcanus II rose to the throne and was king for three months before his brother, Aristobulus II, rebelled. Hyrcanus II possessed the backing of the Pharisees, while Aristobulus II recruited the Sadducees. Hyrcanus II led a military consisting of loyal Pharisees and mercenaries, but his brother had more followers and won the initial conflict outside of Jerusalem.

Hyrcanus II took refuge in Jerusalem, but Aristobulus II forced him out. According to some sources, Hyrcanus II then fled the region and took the wife and children of Aristobulus II hostage, but the two

---

[28] Ibid.

brothers managed to come to an agreement before the situation grew more drastic. Aristobulus II would become the king and High Priest, but Hyrcanus II could retain some of the revenue from the offices and received various dignities as the king's brother. The two men switched houses, with Aristobulus II moving into the palace and Hyrcanus II taking his brother's home.

However, most sources agree that the civil war continued until Rome stepped in. During the civil war, the Roman general Marcus Aemilius Scaurus went to capture Syria and the rest of the Seleucid Empire in the name of Pompey the Great.

Pompey the Great

Pompey the Great was one of the Roman Republic's most successful military commanders and would eventually become part of the infamous First Triumvirate of Rome. Scaurus entered Syria and came upon the civil war between Hyrcanus II and Aristobulus II. Both brothers attempted to gain Scaurus on their side through gifts, promises, and bribes. Originally, Aristobulus II managed to gain Rome's favor through a gift of 400 talents. However, this changed when Pompey the Great himself arrived in Syria. He looked at the two brothers and saw very different, distinct personalities. Aristobulus II was smart, cunning, and militarily experienced while Hyrcanus II was softer, weaker, and more easily controlled.

Pompey the Great earned the nickname "Conqueror of Asia" due to his skills as a general and desired to bring Judea under the control of Rome in order to expand the Republic's territory.[29] Hyrcanus II and Aristobulus II approached the commander with more gifts and promises. Pompey delayed revealing a decision despite receiving truly lavish possessions like a golden vine worth 500 talents. Aristobulus II realized that Pompey intended to bring an end to the civil war by taking over the Hasmonean Dynasty and retreated with his armies. He established a fortress at Alexandrium, but realized that his efforts were fruitless.

To appease Pompey, Aristobulus II decided to hand over Jerusalem. However, the people refused to open the gates to the army and a long siege ensued. When the Romans arrived, Jerusalem was taken by the Roman Republic. Judea came under the control of the Romans and became yet another protectorate that needed to pay tribute and live under the control of a Roman governor.[30]

---

[29] Robin Seager, *Pompey the Great: A Political Biography*, (Blackwell Publishing, 2002).
[30] Richard Hooker, *"The Hebrews: The Diaspora,"* retrieved 2006, World Civilizations Learning Modules, Washington State University, 1999.

Pompey in the Temple of Jerusalem by Jean Fouquet, 1470 CE

Chapter 9 – Roman Rule of Judea

The Hasmonean Dynasty did not crumble immediately when the Romans intervened. Although Judea was now under the rule of a Roman governor, it still had a ruler called an ethnarch, which was a political leader for a specific, homogenous group of people. This role went to Hyrcanus II around 47 BCE after a prolonged struggle between Pompey and Caesar. Pompey the Great continued to support the weak Hyrcanus II as the High Priest while the Roman administrators in the region split the former Hasmonean Kingdom into the territories of Galilee, Samaria, and Judea. Five councils ruled each individual area including Jerusalem and the city of Jericho. Hyrcanus II continued to be denied the role of king and the official control of the region went to a Roman named Antipater.

The Fall of the Hasmonean Dynasty

Hyrcanus II did not enjoy the presence of Antipater. Antipater took away Hyrcanus II's influence and additionally gave his sons powerful appointments such as the governor of Jerusalem or governor of Galilee. Herod, one of Antipater's youngest sons, held the power in Galilee and annoyed Hyrcanus II so greatly that the High Priest forced him under trial for supposed abuses of power. Herod went into exile in 46 BCE but returned only a short time later.

Hyrcanus II

In 44 BCE, the friends of the famous Julius Caesar assassinated him. A Roman civil war ensued during which the generals of rival factions invaded outlying territories such as Syria and Judea. The Parthians, a Roman enemy to the east of the Israelites, also marched into Roman land with the assistance of the former general Quintus Labienus. After dividing its army, the Parthians managed to conquer all of the Levant, including Judea.

Hyrcanus II went with an emissary to talk to the Parthians and establish a form of peace. The Parthians captured him and his companion, chopped off his ears, and held him as a prisoner. The Romans didn't care. A man called Antigonus became the new king and High Priest but failed to eliminate Herod, who vied with Antigonus for power. Herod sought support from Marc Antony, one of the central leaders of Rome. Marc Antony and the Roman Senate declared Herod the true king of the Israelites (called "King of the Jews") and gave him additional forces to fight Antigonus.

The struggle lasted for three years, from 40 BCE to 37 BCE. The majority of the forces from the Romans fought against the Parthians to the east, so Herod was mostly on his own. It wasn't until after the Romans defeated the Parthians that Herod successfully defeated Antigonus and handed him over to Marc Antony, who beheaded the former High Priest. Hasmonean rule came to an end when the Roman Senate officially named Herod the true ruler of Judea.

Herod and Continued Roman Control

Herod would be known as Herod the Great. His official position was as a Roman client king of Judea, or the ruler of a smaller territory who still needs to answer to the Roman Senate. He ruled from 37 BCE to 4 BCE. Many people struggle to classify the king's legacy. While he completed impressive building projects, formed a new aristocracy, and improved the economy of Judea, he also let many of his citizens live in poverty and decried many Jewish customs.

Herod the Great

Herod began what would be known as the Herodian Dynasty, which would be additionally ruled by his sons upon his death. He required consistent support from the Roman Senate to remain in power and dealt with many threats to his throne. In particular, his mother-in-law, Alexandra, sought to regain power for her family, the Hasmoneans. She attempted to convince Marc Antony to make one of her relatives the High Priest. To avoid the issue, Herod ordered his first assassination.[31]

Next, a power struggle in Rome between two powerful leaders, Octavian and Antony, began. Herod sided with Antony in 37 BCE, but Antony lost. Herod wagered his reputation and used it to

---

[31] Adam Kolman Marshak, *The Many Faces of Herod the Great*, (Eerdmans, 2015).

convince Octavian that he would be loyal and keep Judea under control and providing riches to Rome. Octavian allowed Herod to remain in his position. Historians argue what the actual Judeans thought about Herod, with most professionals agreeing that the Judeans didn't like him as a ruler.

Herod spend most of his money on lavish building products like the expansion of the Temple in Jerusalem, new fortresses, and new cities like Caesarea Maritima. He taxed the people heavily to give gifts to influential people within Rome. He further extracted inordinate qualities of asphalt from the Dead Sea for shipbuilding and leased copper mines to improve his wealth.

Although he improved and enhanced the Temple of Jerusalem, Herod received criticism from the majority of the population and even from the Pharisees and Sadducees. He angered the Pharisees by not listening to their recommendations and suggestions on how to work on the Temple. The Sadducees were upset because Herod removed many of their influential priests and officials from their positions and replaced them with gentiles, or non-Jews. To make matters worse, Herod liked to bring in foreign forms of entertainment and constructed a massive golden eagle near the entrance of the Temple, which showed his dedication to Rome.[32]

---

[32] Ibid.

Herod's Burial Site

Herod died in 4 BCE and was buried at a location known as the Herodium. The majority of his kingdom was separated into tetrarchs among Herod's three sons, with part of the territory going to Herod's sister-in-law. One of these tetrarchies was Judea, which included Jerusalem, the former kingdom of Judah, and parts of Samaria and Idumea. Herod's son Herod Archelaus took over Judea and was such a terrible ruler that the Roman emperor actually threw him out of power in 6 CE after the population of Judea literally begged Rome to do something about him.

Control and the Jewish-Roman Wars

It was at this point, 6 CE, that Judea finally came under direct Roman administrative control, not through a king or ruler of the territory as a vassal. Judea did not bring Rome much money, but it controlled influential sea and land routes that connected Rome to Egypt, which was the breadbasket of the region. It also served as a border province which protected Rome from their enemy the

Parthians. Rome divided Judea into five administrative districts: Jerusalem, Gadara, Amathus, Jericho, and Sepphoris.

Judea managed to exist in relative peace under Rome for about six decades before the Jews (Israelites) became discontented and started to revolt. Around 66 CE began the Jewish-Roman Wars. Judea was influential during the first Jewish-Roman War. It lasted from 66 CE-70 CE and resulted in the siege of Jerusalem, the destruction of Herod's Temple (the improved Temple of Jerusalem), and forced Judea under even more control from Rome. The next important conflict was the Bar Kokhba revolt from 132 CE-135 CE. The Jews lost again and the Roman emperor renamed Judea to strip away the Jewish identity.

Over time, the control of Judea would shift from the Romans to a semi-independent state and then back into a destroyed community. The people would form several diasporas as their homeland came under the control of different conquerors. The nomadic lifestyle of the Israelites heavily influenced their religion, which became modern Judaism and which would eventually give rise to Christianity and Islam.

Chapter 10 – Ancient Hebrew Religion and Judaism

The Hebrew or Israelite religion was significant for keeping the early civilization together. According to their beliefs, the Israelites were descended from the same ancestors and served as their god's chosen, making them a significant ethnic group. Religion played a crucial function in everyday life because of the rules and regulations laid down by Yahweh, the chief and eventually singular deity of the Israelites. Among the laws which controlled daily life were:

- A ban on marrying anyone who was not ethnically an Israelite
- The creation of a hereditary priesthood
- A ban on adultery, murder, and theft
- The prohibition on worshipping other gods besides Yahweh
- A ban on the use of images depicting Yahweh

The Israelite religion was complex and changed over time to reflect the growing power of Israel. At its height, the kingdom possessed 300,000 religious followers. One of the biggest transitions was from polytheism to monotheism.

Monotheism vs. Polytheism

The ancient Hebrew religion did not develop until the late Iron Age. Before this period, the Israelites practiced the Canaanite religion, which involved the worship of multiple deities believed to be in control of different aspects of life. This veneration of more than one god is called polytheism. Eventually, the Israelites shifted away from the traditional Canaanite dogma and began to focus more on the worship of ancestors and so-called family gods, or specific deities believed to be related to the welfare of a specific patriarchal line. This transition still followed certain sections of the Canaanite religion, but involved less centralized worship than typically seen at Canaanite centers.

When a clear monarchy established itself during the latter half of the Iron Age, the Israelites gradually shifted to monotheism, or the belief in and worship of a single deity. The monarchy promoted its specific family deity above all others, built temples, and encouraged the people to transition to the worship of this god instead of personal family deities. This god was Yahweh, who was frequently integrated with El, the former chief deity of the Canaanites. Outside of the royal court, though, people continued to be polytheistic and worship their family deities. It wasn't until the full establishment of Judah and Israel and the following Assyrian conquest that the Israelites would fully adopt monotheism and Yahweh.

Yahweh

The story of Yahweh begins in the Bronze Age, when the Israelites weren't yet a distinct group and continued to live in other political states. Scholars are not sure about the exact etymology behind the name "Yahweh," but many believe it was actually another title for the main Canaanite god El, especially since the Israelites used to be Canaanites.[33]

El was the supreme god over all others, the creator of humans and animals. El fathered some of the most important deities in the pantheon, including the gods of storms, death, and the sea. His main designation was as the god of wisdom, the ancient grey-bearded one who controlled the cosmos. He possessed numerous names, one of which was Yahweh, and his primary name, El, was used in Canaanite and Israelite writing to refer to gods in general due to his influence and power.

The theory that El and Yahweh are the same deity is supported by passages found from some of the earliest writings in the Old Testament. For example, a line from the Book of Exodus states that Yahweh revealed himself to Abraham, Isaac, and Jacob as Ēl Shaddāi, and that they did not yet know his true name, YHVH, which was believed to translate to "Yahweh." The Book of Genesis contains similar references, where Abraham accepts the blessing of the god El. However, not everyone believes that El and Yahweh were the same deity, especially since the word El could be used to refer to a god in general.

Whether Yahweh was El or not, what is true is that the Israelite god seemed to be the product of syncretism, or the amalgamation of different religious beliefs into one singular culture or practice. Some modern examples would be how Latin American Catholicism incorporates numerous elements from indigenous religious practices, or Haitian voodoo, which combines African beliefs with Christian elements. The Israelite Yahweh was occasionally referred to as a storm god and is prophesized to one day battle a great leviathan or sea beast, as was done by the Canaanite storm god Ba'al.[34]

---

[33] John Day, *Yahweh and the Gods and Goddesses of Canaan*, (New York: Sheffield Academic Press, 2002).
[34] Ibid.

The Destruction of the Leviathan by Gustave Doré, 1865

The oldest known record of the usage of Yahweh comes from an Egyptian inscription written during the time of Pharaoh Amenhotep III, who lived from 1402 BCE to 1363 BCE. Here, Yahweh appears as part of a place name which reads "land of Shasu of yhw." The Shasu were a group of nomads from northern Arabia who hailed primarily from Edom and Midian, two locations associated with Yahweh in biblical studies. The leading hypothesis in contemporary times is that traders with the nomads gradually introduced the concept of Yahweh to the Canaanites in the south, which was how it spread throughout the Levant during the Bronze Age. Yahweh gradual's conflation with El occurred during the early Iron Age (1200 BCE-930 BCE), and he would eventually become the main deity of Israel and Judah during the late Iron Age (1000 BCE-586 BCE).

A Roman Drachma Depicting Yahweh

By 1000 BCE, Yahweh became the national god of the kingdom of Israel, but not Judah. By all historical accounts, he seemed to only be worshipped in these two places, which was not uncommon for a god at this time. Throughout the Levant, different peoples were turning away from traditional polytheism and instead worshipped national gods. Some examples include Milcom of the Ammonites, Chemosh of the Moabites, and Quas of the Edomites. People viewed the king of Israel as the viceroy of Yahweh on earth, and the king would reinforce this idea by performing a ceremony at Jerusalem each year where Yahweh was enthroned at the temple there. Numerous artists over the centuries have created paintings demonstrating this ceremony, including a famous example from James Tissot.

Solomon at Jerusalem

Israelite Religion and the Assyrians

The distinctive religion found in Jewish and Christian scriptures formed from the ancient Israeli dogma following the Assyrian invasion and destruction of the kingdom of Israel around 722 BCE. Refugees from the north fled to nearby Judah to escape captivity, enslavement, or death. Thousands of Israelites were taken by the Assyrians and relocated, as the Assyrian empire wanted its own people to inhabit the capital and other resource-laden spots throughout the territory. The refugees to Judah brought their worship of Yahweh with them, which was adopted by the wealthy landowners and nobles of the kingdom. The religion spread so quickly that by 640 BCE, the eight-year-old prince Josiah was crowned. By 622 BCE, Josiah and his followers, who all worshipped Yahweh, made a bit for independence against their Assyrian conquerors, during which they proclaimed they were loyal to Yahweh alone and would serve no other master.

Practices

The early Israelites worshipped deities in a similar manner to other ancient peoples. Temples were central to worship and needed to be carefully maintained and cleaned so the deity could live inside. The building's holiness was frequently reinforced and attended to through rituals, liturgy, sacrifices, and offerings. Because the Israelites viewed gods as divine essences, they gave special care to ensure the temple maintained high standards. Originally, men and women would participate in rituals and women were typically responsible for preparing loaves and incense offered to the gods.

Archaeological evidence matches up with writings in the Book of Leviticus, which stated there were five different offerings the Israelites could use, each with three different levels so the rich and poor alike could give something significant. The five offerings were burnt, grain, wellbeing, sin, and guilt. If someone needed to give a burnt offering, they could choose from the level that corresponded with their economic class:

- Wealthy: Bull
- Middle: Sheep or goat
- Poor: Pigeon or turtledove

A Standard Pigeon

It was important for the ancient Israelites to offer a proper sacrifice or gift based on their economic class, so wealthy individuals could not get away with only giving a pigeon.

Divination was another significant religious practice. In ancient times, divination was the practice of raising or speaking to the dead in order to learn information or predict the future. Although some places condemned it as necromancy, sources indicate the Israelites and Judeans practiced divination regularly. However, this ritual did not have a stable place in religious practice. It seems like some holidays and temples encouraged divination while others explicitly banned it as sorcery, making divination a highly controversial practice for many people.

Finally, the Israelites celebrated numerous holidays and festivals through choreographed rituals. One important holiday was the Day of Atonement, when the Israelites believed Yahweh abandoned the temple due to the sins of the worshippers. A high priest needed to make sacrifices to atone for the sins of the Israelites and then sprinkle the blood upon Yahweh's altar. The final step was to transfer the people's sinfulness to a goat, which would then be burnt as a form of cleansing the people and Yahweh's sanctuary of all of the sin built up over the year. Like many other populations, the Israelites additionally celebrated the changing of the seasons through rituals, such as Passover and the New Moon festivals.

Conclusion

The Israelites continue to be one of the most well-documented ancient peoples in the world due to their impact on contemporary Western society, religion, and culture. Without the Israelites, it's unlikely that the three Abrahamic religions–Judaism, Christianity, and Islam–would exist.

Jewish Star of David, Christian Cross and the Islamic Word for "Allah"

Many other historical events would also have turned out differently if the Israelites did not endure and move out of the Levant into other areas around the world, including Northern Africa, Europe, and parts of Asia Minor. During medieval and modern times, the Israelites gradually turned into the contemporary Jewish population, just as other former Israelites became Christians or even Muslims that spread their religions throughout Europe, Asia, North America, South America, Australia, and Africa.

The former Israelites have contributed magnificently to science, mathematics, art, modern Hollywood, and to the cultures of dozens of countries. Without the Israelites, many events and inventions, both good and bad, might never have come to pass. For example, contemporary Israel, the tragedy of the Holocaust, stainless steel, the famous theory of relativity, color television, or the atomic bomb.

It's difficult for people to comprehend just how connected humans are to their ancestors from the past, and the Israelites are a prime example. One of the main reasons why humans possess so much knowledge about these people is because their descendants continued to live and adapt to new environments; they recorded their history, and maintained their religion. Without the Israelites, modern society would not be the same.

Read more Captivating History Books about Ancient History

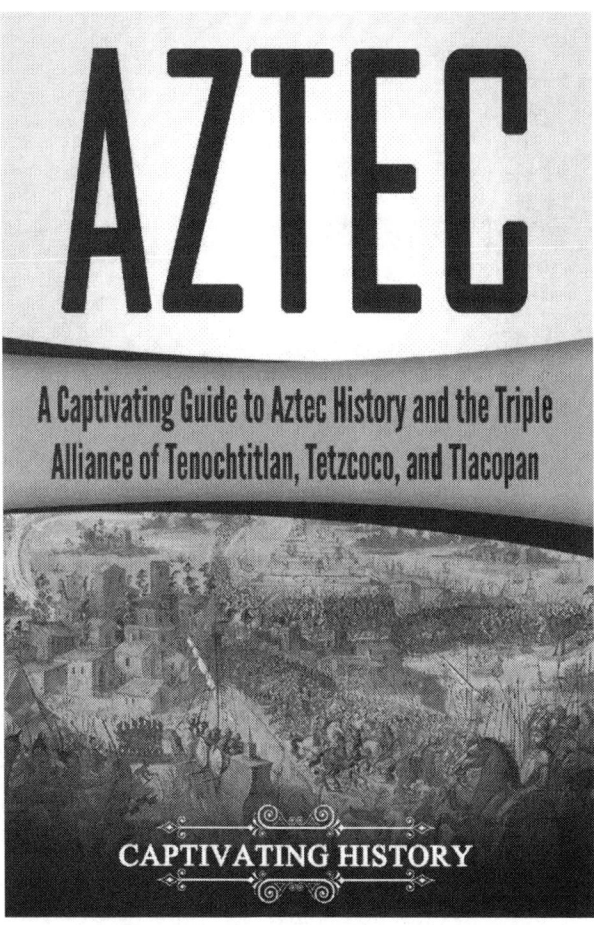

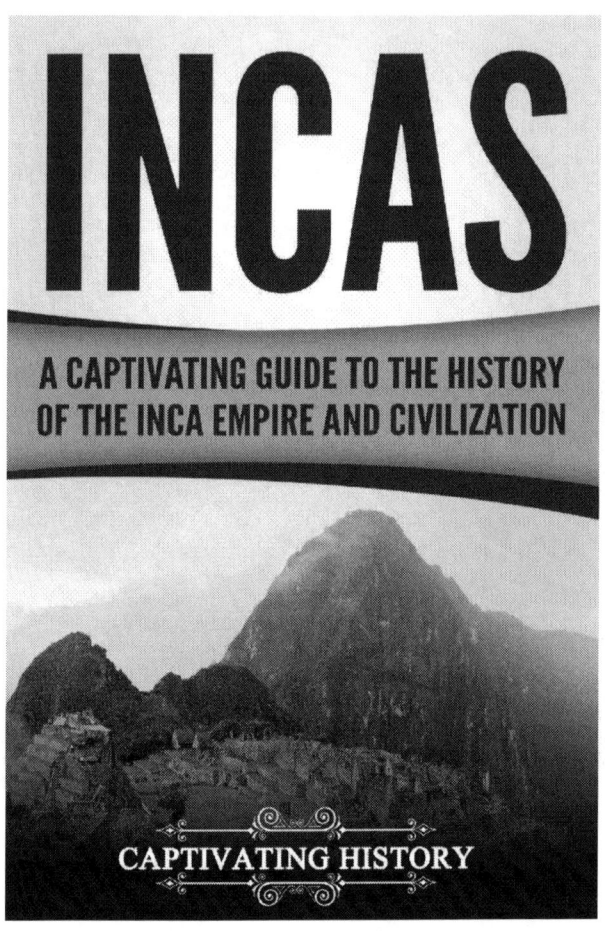

Bibliography

Albertz, Rainer (2003). *Israel in Exile: The History and Literature of the Sixth Century B.C.E.* Society of Biblical Literature.

Cline, Eric H. (2014). *1177 B.C.: The Year Civilization Collapsed.* New Jersey: Princeton University Press.

Cornfled, Gaalyahu. (1962). *Daniel to Paul: Jews In Conflict with Graeco-Roman Civilization.* New York: The Macmillan Company

Coogan, Michael D. (2009). *A Brief Introduction to the Old Testament.* Oxford University Press.

Day, John. (2002). *Yahweh and the Gods and Goddesses of Canaan.* New York: Sheffield Academic Press.

Goodspeed, George Stephen. (2014). *A History of the Babylonians and Assyrians.* Independent Publishing.

Grant, Michael. (1984). *The History of Ancient Israel.* Scribner.

Hooker, Richard. *"The Hebrews: The Diaspora".* Retrieved 2006. World Civilizations Learning Modules. Washington State University, 1999.

Kolman Marshak, Adam. (2015). *The Many Faces of Herod the Great.* Eerdmans.

Lipovsky, Igor P. (2017) *Judea Between Two Eras.* Boston: Cambridge Publishing, Inc.

MacDonald, Nathan. (2008). *What Did the Ancient Israelites Eat?: Diet in Biblical Times.* Grand Rapids: Wm. B. Eerdmans Publishing Co.

Martin, Thomas R. and Blackwell, Christopher W. (2012). *Alexander the Great: The Story of an Ancient Life.* New York: Cambridge University Press.

Miller, J. Maxwell. (2006). *A History of Ancient Israel and Judah, Second Edition* Louisville: Westminster John Knox Press.

Rogerson, J. W. (2006). *The Oxford Handbook of Biblical Studies.* OUP Oxford. p. 292.

Seager, Robin. (2002). *Pompey the Great: A Political Biography.* Blackwell Publishing.

Sievers, Joseph and Neusner, Jacob ed. (1990) *The Hasmoneans and Their Supporters: From Matthias to the Death of John Hyrcanus I.* Atlanta.: Scholars Press.

Sparks, Kenton L. (1998). *Ethnicity and Identity in Ancient Israel.* Eisenbrauns.

Waters, Matt. (2014). *Ancient Persia: A Concise History of the Achaemenid Empire, 550-330 BCE.* New York: Cambridge University Press.

Worthington, Ian. (2016). *Ptolemy I: King and Pharaoh of Egypt.* New York: Oxford University Press.

Made in the USA
Lexington, KY
29 December 2018